*Mind your
Own business*

Mind Your Own Business

Mind Your Own Business

Lessons from a Hardworking Restaurateur

Tommy Brann

with Side Dishes from Brian VanOchten

FREEZE■FRAME
publishing

freezeframepublishing.com

Mind Your Own Business

All rights reserved. Published 2013. Freeze Frame Publishing, 10383 36th Street, Lowell, MI. Printed at Color House Graphics, Grand Rapids, Michigan in the United States of America.

Cover design Amy Cole, JPL Design Solutions.

Cover photo originally appeared in The Grand Rapids Press edition of MLive on July 24, 2011. All rights reserved. Used with permission of MLive and The Grand Rapids Press.

For information about special discounts on bulk purchases, please contact Mr. Brann at tombrann@branns.com.

Mr. Brann is available to speak to your class, club, group or organization. Please contact him at tombrann@branns.com.

For more information on Branns Steakhouse and Sports Grille
   www.branns.com
   www.facebook.com/branns
   www.facebook.com/tommy.brann

Library of Congress Control Number: 2013945956

ISBN 978-0-9839868-5-0

Dedication

To my wife Sue
and all of the dogs in our life that provided love
in my journey in the restaurant business.
To John and Liz Brann
my dad and mom.
~t.b.

To my sister, Jody Lynn VanOchten,
and my nephew, Patrick David Daneluk,
you are both forever in my heart.
I miss you each and every minute of
each and every day.

~b.v.o.

Table of Contents

Foreword

I was barely out of kindergarten when I started my first business taking out trash for other residents of the apartment complex in which my family lived. I didn't know I was entrepreneurial then, but looking back, that was clearly the beginning. My father's job with Ford Motor Company took our family all over the world. When I came back to the United States for college in the early 1980's, I had no idea what I wanted to do with my life, but I was determined to pay my own way through Michigan State University. I found a job working at a family restaurant as a dishwasher, then moved up the ladder to prep cook, line cook, head cook and assistant manager. By the time I graduated with a degree in Hospitality Business, I was running the restaurant, and my love affair with the food service industry was born. Within a few years, I owned one of those family restaurants, after helping the owners grow the concept from one to four units.

The taste of that early success was gratifying, but there was still something tugging at my soul... a desire to develop my own concept. And so, on March 15, 1995, that dream came to fruition with the opening of the first *Beaner's Cup-A-Cino* in East Lansing, Michigan, a specialty coffee shop with an uncomplicated and welcoming style that puts a fun twist on serving the world's best coffee.

In the beginning, I was a shop-keeper, working 16-hour days, trying to rub two pennies together to make a nickel. It was a rough start and I almost went out of business, but with focus, creativity, and the sheer force of will, it began to take off. Together with my two great business partners, we opened a second location in 1997, and began franchising in 1999. We changed our name to *Biggby Coffee* in 2006, and today we have 182 locations in 9 states, and we keep on growing!

I met Tommy Brann as a board member of the Michigan Restaurant Association (MRA). I became a board member when our concept only had 5 locations and, frankly, I didn't think that I was qualified. I almost turned the invitation down, but in the end, in spite of being apprehensive, the opportunity to sit should-to-shoulder with so many of the larger-than-life icons of the Michigan restaurant industry that I had read about in school was too exciting to resist.

One of those icons was Tommy Brann, a true Michigan legend. Out of all the people that I met in my many years at the MRA, he is the one that has left the longest lasting impression.

The charm of meeting Tommy is that whether you met him today, yesterday, or ten years ago, he never changes. I watched many board members get carried away with a sense of self-importance, and become people I couldn't recognize, but Tommy always stays true. He has unparalleled integrity, humility, passion, and honesty. Simply put, Tommy is the kind of person who can restore your faith in the goodness of humanity. In all the years we served together on the MRA Board, he always brought out the best in all of us and he served the restaurant industry with dignity and respect. When Tommy was eventually 'termed out,' the board unanimously granted him 'Honorary' status, which means he became a board member for life. I feel blessed to have crossed paths with him.

Mind Your Own Business is a heartfelt chronicle of life's lessons and how they influence the great journey of owning a business. I have always felt that business success is not innate, and that the sum total of life experiences plays such a large role in smart business intuition. This book is the perfect insight into how your life values influence the kind of person you become, and how that in turn influences success in your business, your community, and your family.

I knew Tommy, the legend and colleague, before I read this book. Now I know Tommy the man. It's a good story with hard truths, and I guarantee if you read this book, you'll feel good when you're done...and you'll be a whole lot wiser.

Bob Fish
Co-Founder/CEO
Biggby Coffee
East Lansing, Michigan, 2013

Acknowledgements

I want to thank Brian VanOchten for helping me get over the mountain on this book. I want to thank my employees, some who have been with me over 30 years, for their dedication and friendship. To my partners in business, Mike Brann, Johnny Brann, and Tom Doyle, for understanding what we go through as a small business. The Michigan Restaurant Association, for sticking up for us against the forces that do not understand the sacrifices we make as restaurant owners. My fellow restaurant friends, I know you work so hard. My nephew, Johnny Jr., who has been a good sounding board for my book. All the small businesses in this country and the people that have that entrepreneurial spirit in them, whether they succeed or fail, I understand you. To John Galt, who I am looking forward to having a Brann's Sizzlin' Steak with.

And last, my dogs, Spinoza, Bo, Millie, Muddy, Jake, and Casey who have passed away but are dear to us and buried under our bedroom window. To Howie, our 14 year old dog who provides us with love, and brings tears to my eyes as I type this.

Tommy's Lessons

1. *Treat your small business like a baby.*
   (Chapter 10)

2. *It's never too late to learn something new.*
   (Chapter 3)

3. *Focus on your core business.* (Chapter 2)

4. *You can say it's not personal, but it is.*
   (Chapter 6)

5. *Follow through. Details are important.*
   (Chapter 4)

6. *React swiftly to problems.* (Chapter 1)

7. *Let your successes inspire you during difficult times.* (Chapter 1)

8. *You always have to evolve. If you don't, you're going to sink.* (Chapter 15)

9. *Sometimes it feels like you're the only one that 'gets' it.* (Chapter 12)

10. *Complexity can kill a business.* (Chapter 14)

11. *Don't let your emotions make your business decisions.* (Chapter 8)

12. *A little paranoia is a good thing.* (Chapter 9)

13. *The word BUSINESS is not a cold word.*
   (Chapter 9)

"Life is what happens while you're busy making other plans."
—*John Lennon*

Chapter 1:
Dirty Dishes

I first started minding my own business as a teenager.

The phrase "mind your own business" had a double meaning for me in the late 1960s when I became part of the family restaurant business, busing tables at my father's establishment at age 16, and later as the youngest restaurant owner in the state of Michigan when I opened my own restaurant at age 19 in 1971. All teenagers are told by elders, especially their parents, to mind their own business at times, but I learned through small-business ownership and free enterprise that minding my own business isn't just solid advice for adolescents preparing to make the leap into adulthood. It is the same guiding principle that has made me the proud owner of one of Grand Rapids' favorite family restaurant chains.

Shortly after graduating from East Grand Rapids High School, when most of my teenage friends were preparing to go off to college or begin looking for jobs in the real world, I opened Tommy Brann's Sizzling Steaks and Sports Grille, 4157 S. Division Ave., in Wyoming. Following in my father's footsteps, and with his encouragement and support, I launched a restaurant, and embarked on a tireless pursuit that would span my lifetime. On top of signing up for a career of 24/7 hard labor for the next 40 or 50 years, I was also unknowingly investing myself in a business decision that would teach me new lessons over and over again until they sunk in.

It didn't require nearly as much growing up as you might think to prepare me to run a business at 19. I still had a lot to learn but not all of those lessons were difficult to understand, though; some came easy. For instance, the first important lesson learned that helped shape my early years of small-business ownership was self-discipline.

Part of why I took so naturally to this lesson was because I had already been learning it for years. At 16 years old, I started working at my dad's restaurant, John Brann's Steakhouse, 2053 S. Division Ave., in Grand Rapids, in 1961. You learn self-discipline pretty quickly when your father is the guy who signs your paychecks. In addition to teaching me some responsibility, working for my dad kept me out of trouble as well. I played football at East Grand Rapids, which helped me develop discipline in my life, but I still hung around friends who were experimenting with drugs, which was very much a part of the culture in the late 1960s and early '70s. I just as easily could have gone down that same path, but my dad put me to work at his restaurant and thus my lifelong journey into small business began.

The not-so-glamorous job of busing tables at John Brann's Steakhouse was exhausting, but necessary work and a natural beginning to my small-business career. I was an adolescent mixture of bashfulness and cockiness, both part of my character as a typical teenager searching for his place in the real world, but I found that it didn't take long to gain respect from both the staff and our customers. I worked hard and found that if I did my job and kept my mouth shut, people would be bragging about me to my dad, which was the ultimate reward. It felt good to hear staff and customers praising me to my father.

I loved my dad. He was fun to work for, but being the boss' son made me uncomfortable at times. To this day, I really don't like people making a big deal about me being the owner of Tommy Brann's Sizzling Steaks and Sports Grille. At 16, when I first started, I felt the staff at my father's place doing this, but, fortunately, they got over it after a few weeks, and I was accepted as just "Tommy the busboy."

I was not Tommy the busboy for very long.

That's when dish washing became part of my life. I truly believe this is still the toughest and most unappreciated job in the restaurant business. It did not deter me, though, because I found a sense of surprising and immense pride in it. I constantly strived to be the best dishwasher in West Michigan.

Looking back, washing dishes was sort of a micro-model for small business ownership. At many small restaurants it's often a one-person station, so it can be what you make of it. You can slack off or you can make it your own, innovate the system and hone your technique. That's what I did when I was in that position and I took pride in knowing that if the result of my effort was good I could take all the credit, but if the result was bad I had to take all the blame. Although it may seem like a menial job, it's actually crucial to the entire operation. If the dishes aren't there to serve the food on, everything grinds to a halt, which means that everyone is relying on you. Even then I really loved the challenge of that responsibility.

It also taught me that that a small business can and should react swiftly to problems and solutions. Anytime a waitress or busboy would bring water glasses back to the kitchen to us dishwashers, they would yell, "Glasses!" It meant we had to grab them from the tables right away and get them washed. Most of the time in the restaurant industry there's no time to sit and debate about how to address a situation. There's a need and you fill it, there's a problem and you fix it, right then and there. The problem: dirty glasses. The solution: immediately wash them.

I have a lot of fond memories of my teenage years working for my dad. As I mentioned, spending time at the restaurant helped to keep me out of trouble and so did playing football for East Grand Rapids High School. I learned an important lesson from both.

I went out for football my freshman year. It taught me about discipline, showing up on time, establishing good habits in practice, and following orders.

I remember one practice in particular which left a lasting impression on me about the importance of discipline and the power that it has to open the door to opportunity and success. I was the second-string right guard and I missed one practice when I had to go to the dentist. In that same practice, the first-string right guard kept screwing up and the coaches kept calling my name: "Brann!" I was being summoned to replace the starting right guard. It's the only practice I missed all year, and it really stung to hear from my teammates that I had missed that opportunity to move up in the ranks and show what I could do. I didn't get reprimanded for my absence because I had a valid excuse, but I was right back at second-string the next day.

It reinforces the importance of timing in business – and all aspects of life. Self-discipline isn't just about good or bad. Working hard and showing up every day is a practice that results in very real opportunities for success. If you are always there, doing the work, you won't be able to miss the good things that come your way. It's a way of sort of making your own luck.

I had to wait until my sophomore year to move up to first-string defensive back. I liked playing on defense because you're more free to do things. Once the play starts you can choose to stay on your man or blitz the quarterback or go for an interception. I'm a guy who likes to have choices and one of the biggest things that owning your own business affords you is the freedom to make your own decisions. You can be an entrepreneur. You can innovate and try new things. I liked that on the football field and I loved it in my job.

I'll never forget my first and only interception in high school football. It happened against Godwin Heights at East Grand Rapids in 1968. I went back, guarded the receiver, and kept him in front of me. The pass slipped out of his hands. I couldn't have dropped the ball if I had wanted to. It fell right into my hands and I ran 20 yards or so after picking it off. I'm not sure if my eyes were open, but I still ran it back. It showed me how your natural instincts sometimes take over. Despite my surprise and excitement when I caught that ball, my instincts kicked in and I even managed to run it in the right direction and everything. It was a big highlight for me then and still an extremely proud memory for me today.

I think it's very important to remember your successes in life. If you can remind yourself of your past accomplishments they can serve as inspiration and help you through difficult times.

Playing football kept me on the straight and narrow but that wasn't the case for many of my teammates. A lot of guys got kicked off our football team during the season for drinking, but I wasn't one of them.

During my junior and senior years, the friends I'd hang around, like Rick and Gary, ended up getting into trouble. Gary was a really cool guy with long blond hair, a good-looking guy; he had a beard and the girls just magnetized to him. The problem is that Gary used drugs, and Rick used drugs and drank too much as well.

I'm especially proud of the fact that I kept myself clean because in many ways it was a very difficult time. My mom, Elizabeth, died when I was 13, and it would have been very easy for me to turn to drugs and alcohol to deal with the pain of that loss. My dad, in his wisdom, got me working in his restaurant at 15, and that was a gift the set my life on the right path in more ways than one. The structure it provided me was crucial at that time when the inherent structure of our family had been altered so drastically by the loss of my mother. Of course it was also the beginning of my education in restaurant management which laid the foundation for my future career. It also taught me a lot of self-reliance and the value of independence. I actually moved out of the house at age 17 and lived in the apartment above his restaurant at Burton and Division in Burton Heights. I was on my own, but I still had the stabilizing presence of my dad's place and the work I did there.

My work and living situation also allowed me to be a safety net for my friends who hadn't managed to stay out of trouble as much as I had. My friend Rick got kicked out of his house because he had some problems. His father was a good doctor, but he couldn't take it anymore. So, Rick lived with me. He was like my housekeeper. He kept the place clean. At the time I thought that living with me had had a positive effect on Rick, but what I didn't know was that, while I was working, my friends were doing drugs in my apartment, and not just marijuana. Some heavy drugs. I didn't even know a lot of this stuff was happening because I was working all the time. I felt bad for them when I found out what was going on, and looking back on it I felt very grateful for my dad's wisdom from being in small business and free enterprise, which went a long way in keeping me out of trouble.

I really loved work. I loved to accomplish things. I loved to please my dad perhaps most of all. It's what started my small-business enterprise and I learned all about what small businesses go through to achieve success.

During my senior year in high school, my friend had a small-enterprise system he was experimenting with himself. What he would do was go to Jacobson's clothing store in East Grand Rapids and other clothing stores. He would go in there and try stuff on, putting his old clothes over the new clothes and walk out without paying. Then he'd sell those items. I'm ashamed to admit he sold some of them to me and he'd sell the stuff to other friends. It was a little enterprise, but of course it was a dishonest one. I don't know if he ever got caught, but, after owning my own small business for about 20 years I did the right thing and I manned up to the situation: I sent Jacobson's, which was still there at the time, a $100 check, certified without my name on it.

I guess I sort of half-manned up. I didn't put my name on the check, but I sent them $100 and wrote the following in a note that I sent with it: "This is for something that happened in my high school years where I bought clothes from somebody."

I credit that integrity move to the influence that small business had on me. I started to appreciate what goes into running a privately owned, small company and began to understand that those were people who were stolen from, not some nameless, heartless corporation. I also learned from watching how my dad treated problems that it's possible to correct mistakes. I did something to correct that one.

Side Dish

Bumps, Bruises and a Black Belt

Tommy Brann refuses to brag about earning a black belt in karate.

It took him nearly twice as long as the average person to reach that prestigious rank since operating a restaurant is an all-consuming lifestyle that doesn't permit a lot of spare time for hobbies or much else.

Yet, through bumps, bruises, and determination, he achieved his goal.

"Yeah, I'm a black belt in karate," he said sheepishly, "but that doesn't mean I'm a great black belt. I'm no Chuck Norris. It took me 7½ years to accomplish it. I would do it right before lunch hour – there was a class from about 10 to 11 a.m. I persevered, I missed very few classes, and even though it takes four years for normal people and it took me 7½ years, I'm still proud of that accomplishment. I don't profess to be the greatest black belt in the world, but I didn't give up. That's a lesson I learned in life. It's a lesson that I applied to being a small-business owner."

In his 42 years as an entrepreneur, he has endured more than his share of frustrating experiences.

"If the toilets overflow on Mother's Day, something bad happens with a party of 20, people don't show up for work or a dishwasher walks out, I'll admit I have walked around my building in frustration, but I never gave up in difficult times. I regrouped instead and fought it head-on. Sometimes you just have to persevere."

It's that sort of fighting spirit that he relied upon to finish second in a karate tournament.

"Here's an example of how bad I was or how good I was as a black belt. Or maybe both. I competed in some tournaments and I won some first-place prizes," he recalled, "but during this one tournament, I didn't win a single match and still finished in second place. I even got my nose broken in this tournament. It bled all over.

"I didn't win one match in that tournament because I kept getting hit so much from illegal contact. If you hit somebody without control, you get disqualified. So, I kept winning my matches and I finished second. Now, is that bragging? Heck no. It's a lesson that you can take your lumps and still get back up."

He still smiles about the abuse he suffered in that tournament.

"It wasn't like Karate Kid. I still laugh about it. It's nothing to brag about," he insisted, "but it shows that I'm a guy who was an average student growing up and I'm an average guy now, but, if you work hard in America, you still can accomplish a lot of good things. You're going to get knocked down in life from time to time, but it's more important to keep getting back up and keep working hard."

"The man who will use his skill and constructive imagination to see how much he can give for a dollar, instead of how little he can give for a dollar, is bound to succeed."
—Henry Ford

Chapter 2:
Paying My Own Way

In high school, I earned C averages as a student, but I never lost focus, and what I lacked in natural ability I made up for with hard work. Unlike a lot of people, I never wanted a free ride. I don't think it's a mark of character as much as stubborn pride; I never wanted anyone to be able to say that I didn't earn my keep.

My dad never treated me with kid gloves either. One summer, he sent me to Charlie's Conditioning Camp, run by an ex-marine up north. I went from the cool comfort of my dad's air-conditioned restaurant to a week of exercising countless hours a day in the heat and humidity. It was tough. This was at a time when there were no water breaks for football players because that was looked upon by the coaches as a sign of weakness. Instead they would give us salt pills during practice. I still remember that someone almost died during one of our training sessions. It was all about old-school discipline at that camp. My dad sent me to it, not because I was a bad kid, but I think because he saw my ambition. I think he saw it as a way to keep me active and keep me focused.

Although I wasn't a star student, I put a lot of effort into working for my father and playing on my high school football team, and I focused even more of my time on those activities after my mom's death.

What I remember most about her death is hearing her screaming, I thought it was just a bad nightmare. I didn't go to school for a couple of weeks afterward. It was hard. My dad was really a great leader and he was a common-sense person, but it was hard on him too. We didn't have in-depth talks about her death or whether I was surrounded by bad influences in high school; I wasn't a troubled kid. It would have been easy for me to deal with the pain of her passing by turning to drugs and alcohol, but I think instead I dealt with it by trying to support my dad, and prove to myself and everyone else that I wasn't broken. I never intended to fill her shoes, but I knew that my dad could use my help then more than ever, and I was at the perfect age to start taking on more responsibility at his restaurant.

I didn't get to skip any of the steps, though. I worked every position that exists in the restaurant business and started off at the bottom just like everybody else. Washing dishes is really an unappreciated job, but I took a lot of pride in scrubbing pots and pans and making sure everything came out sanitized and ready to go. It was actually a nice change of pace after a long day at school, to roll up my sleeves and forget about everything else for a while. As a shy young man it was a good job for me to start with, because I could work alone, just me and my thoughts, but I also knew that I was part of the team. I think it's important to appreciate every position because you've done them all. Every job at a restaurant has valuable lessons to be learned from it. As a bartender I had to deal with money, and giving out change to people isn't automatic when you're a teenager and the customers are adults. I needed both my school education and the little tricks of the trade that I was taught by older co-workers. I learned that if you take a $10 bill, you put it on top of the till and you give the change back to the customer. That way if they said, "No, I gave you a $20 bill," I'd say, "No sir, the 10 dollar bill you gave me is right here on top of the register." Every position I worked had little lessons like that, and a lot of them are useful tools that I've carried with me for the rest of my life.

After my stint as a dishwasher and bus boy, I worked my way up to being a cook and finally a bartender. I was never the manager at John Brann's Steakhouse, but I was always there. If I saw Dick, the bartender, over-pouring, I'd tell him. I know I was a 17-year-old kid, but I'd speak up when it came to work. It wasn't out of arrogance; I wanted my dad's business to do well. I was actually quite bashful. I think if I had a little more cockiness and a little less bashfulness earlier on as a teenager, I might have excelled more in high school and earned higher grades.

I quickly began to develop that confidence as a small-business employee. Working in the restaurant and gaining some responsibility really helped me to come out of my shell. The restaurant business has a way of bringing that out in people. I don't think I would have had the same experience if I'd come into it as a manager right away. Starting off as lowest man on the totem pole made me eager to prove myself. When I moved up in the ranks I knew that I had earned that responsibility, and it gave me a sense of pride that I'd never felt before.

I never turned my nose up at any work that needed to be done, though. I remember one time, Willie, who worked as a cook for my dad, got in some trouble. It was his job to clean up before opening and after close, but he had to miss work so I took over his cleanup duties. I'd sometimes be there from 8 in the morning until 10 p.m. or midnight as a teenager. It might sound sappy, but one thing about small business, is that you get to know the people you work with extremely well, and they sometimes become like your family. Sometimes you see those people more than your wife or your brothers. They looked out for me and vice versa, and of course, at the end of the day, I knew that helping out my coworkers ultimately meant that I was helping out my dad.

My dad helped me out a lot too, but I never wanted to be the silver-spoon kid. I had customers that always said, "Boy, your kid works hard." That felt so good to me because I never wanted anyone to think I had been spoiled because of my dad's success.

As long as I can remember he always liked Ford Thunderbirds, and when I was about sixteen he updated to a new one and gave me his old '65. It was probably about six years old, but to me it seemed really fancy. During my time as a busboy, I'd save my paychecks in a drawer. I didn't cash my father's checks, and sometimes I didn't even punch in on the time clock because I wanted my dad to do well in his business.

Although my understanding of "profit" was probably limited, I felt like making those sacrifices for the family business was the right thing to do, so when my dad gave me his Thunderbird, I thought, "Well, this is silver spoon." I thought a lot about it and I decided to take all of those checks that had been sitting in the drawer and give them to my dad. I wanted to do something to show my appreciation for that car.

He said to me, "Are you sure?"

I was sure, and I still feel good that I did that. I'm not trying to be a martyr, because there was a mere $300 worth of checks there, but I still wanted to pay for the Thunderbird.

Years later I learned that my friend and roommate, Rick, actually made a key to my car, my Thunderbird. He didn't have a car, so he used my car all the time without me even knowing it. I focused so much of my time and energy on the restaurant that I didn't even notice my car missing.

I always wanted to earn my own way, and after proving that I could do any job that the restaurant industry could throw at me, I started to think about how I could do more. My experience working my way up the chain is an example of the free market working at its best. One of the things that's so great about this country is that you can really grow here. I started at the bottom of the ladder and in just a few short years I ended up owning my own restaurant. It should be noted that I was probably a little more focused than the average teenager...maybe even a little too focused. I had paid attention, and I learned one valuable lesson after another from being around my father's restaurant – important lessons that better prepared me to take the next big step forward in my small-business career.

I'll never forget going to Central Bank in Burton Heights and looking over this woman's shoulder while we were waiting in line. It's probably not the right thing to do, to be looking over her shoulder, but I couldn't help it. When I saw that she had $10,000 in her account I thought, "Wow! I want to do that! I want to have that much money in my account someday."

Little impressions like that and seeing the way my dad was growing his business snowballed into me buying life insurance, which is kind of weird for an 18-year-old. I bought two policies, one from Travelers and one from Prudential. I ended up with $100,000 of life insurance at an age when it seemed like I would never die, so I guess I was a little ahead of the game. As much as I always wanted to earn things for myself, I'm proud of the traits I share with my dad and I'm grateful for the opportunities that were opened to me by being his son. Thanks to him I was able to spend a lot of time around business people, and I'd found it to be a really positive experience. I saw the life insurance as sort of a forced savings account, and purchasing those policies was the real beginning of my life as a business man. I started to think about investing in myself, and how I could get other people to invest in me too.

SIDE DISH
The Love Shacks

Upon purchasing the old Southern Restaurant, Tommy Brann inherited some additional structures on his property – a 10-unit motel running along Division Avenue and three cabins behind the motel.

He ran both the restaurant and lodging operations for a while before focusing entirely on his restaurant.

"I've been at this location for 42 years. In 1971, when I started here, I had a 10-unit motel and three cabins right behind the motel units. They were on the north side of the property all lined up in a row," he recalled. "The cabins were brick and had phones and bathrooms, like the little motel unit."

All of that came with the purchase of the property.

He got tired, however, of trying to run both the restaurant and motel.

"The motel units were part of the business, but they became more of a hassle to me – from people not paying rent to it being another business I had to run. It might be a business lesson to focus on your core business. I guess I had a little Steve Jobs in me because I got rid of those motel units and focused on my restaurant business," he said. "It wasn't my focus or something that I knew. My main focus was the restaurant business and that's enough. I got rid of them about four or five years later."

The cabins had a special nickname all to themselves.

"I was 19 or 20 years old at the time when I purchased the property and still a little naïve towards life, but a few of my regular customers had, uh, some particular needs. You could rent a cabin for $1,250 for the whole year, and some of them made it into, you could call it, their own little love shack for their girlfriends," he explained.

He and one of the occupants of the love shack had a good laugh after Brann decided to demolish the motel and cabins to make room for additional parking spaces for restaurant customers.

"I forgot that I was actually renting it out to him and I needed more parking and I wanted to clean up these motels, so I destroyed them. I took them down. It didn't take long. I remember myself throwing some rocks through the widows for fun," he said. "One night, one of the cabin renters pulls up in the dark with his mistress in the car. He gets out of the car and he's got his key and he's looking for the love shack, but it's not there. I remember him telling me that story and we both just laughed at it."

"You've got to say, 'I think that if I keep working at this and want it badly enough, I can have it.'
It's called perseverance."
—Lee Iacocca

Chapter 3:
All in the Family

It was a real family affair at my father's restaurant, and I learned just as much about business from my mother as I did from him.

I think the most important lesson I learned from my parents was the value of hard work. My mother and father often had different ways of approaching business decisions, but one thing they definitely had in common was their work ethic. Her parents raised her to respect the value of a hard day's work, just as my father's family had done with him, and I like to think that they did a good job of instilling that in me. My father was involved in every aspect of the restaurant and he spent most of his time there, but even with four children to care for and a home to run, my mother found a way to be there almost as much as he did. She had her own unique talents that she brought to running the business. My dad always said my mom had a special knack for hiring good servers. In a short conversation she was able to tell from their personalities who would be right for the job.

She also had a way of teaching me things that was different from anyone else I've known. Once, when I was about 11 years old, I was helping my mother in the kitchen and when I took a knife from the drawer, she warned me to be careful, as most mothers would. I shrugged it off, saying, "These knives aren't that sharp!" Of course, I ended up cutting myself and I'll never forget, she started laughing. It wasn't a deep cut or life-threatening, but it tickles me to think about her reaction. I was an 11-year-old who thought he knew better, and my mother knew enough to let me learn from my own mistakes. That was her way. If you think you know better, fine, try it your way. I'll be there to help you get back up when you fall, but I'm going to get a laugh out of it all the same.

My mother led by example, and even in the final stages of her life she was still teaching valuable lessons through her actions.

I remember her first car was a black 1962 Ford Falcon with no power steering. She wanted to learn to drive because that's freedom, so my dad traded in the Falcon for a compact car. It was black with red interior, and she loved that little car. She was already in her late 30s when she decided to learn how to drive, but she did it. That takes a lot of guts. She didn't have to preach or get on a soap box in order to teach me that it's never too late to do things in life. When I'm confronted with a new skill to learn or an opportunity to branch out into something new, I remember my mom getting behind the wheel of that little car and I think, "why not give it a try."

Without her fearless attitude my family might not have achieved the successes that we have. My mother understood the risks of being in the restaurant business, but she always supported my father. He was a good leader, but she was a good leader, too, and I don't think he could have made it through those early years without her wisdom, hard work, and dedication.

Just last year, my cousin passed along to me some letters that my mother wrote way back when they were first starting out with a new business and their first child, me. They would later go on to have great success with the restaurant and have four more children, but they didn't know that then and they were understandably a little scared, uncertain of what the future would hold for them.

In one of the letters my mother wrote to her brother saying, "Sorry, Al, I haven't been able to talk to you, but this is overwhelming," and "please say a prayer for us."

It showed her concern for our family and the pressure they felt after investing everything they had into their own business, not knowing if they would sink or swim. It also showed how much of the burden she carried, never passing off her worries onto anyone else. As children we never felt the weight of the risk my parents were taking in opening a business; they had faith that if we worked hard as a family it would pay off in the end, and as children we felt secure in their certainty.

Included in that card to my Uncle Al was her feelings about her role as a new mother. I was a little kid at the time, and she wrote about how much I'd meant to her as a little baby and being the first of five children. As touching as it was for me to read about how much she loved being my mother, what she wrote about their struggles and how overwhelmed they were is dear to my heart because it shows that she believed in my father, in our family, and in the business, despite the risk.

Regardless of their financial situation, my parents always found a way to keep up certain standards of professionalism. For my father, part of being a business owner meant looking the part. As long as I knew him, my dad wore white shirts and ties. He'd even get dressed up, wearing a white shirt and a suit coat for casual occasions, like a Detroit Tigers baseball game or a family gathering. He was dapper. I never got into that. I'm the opposite. I throw on an apron at work and still manage to come home with stains on my clothes from being in the kitchen. Of course the nature of the industry has changed in some ways since my father's time. The role of the restaurant owner back then was being more of a host, greeting people at the door with a handshake and going table to table chatting with customers or behind the bar. I run my place a little differently. I've gotten my hands a lot dirtier, but at the time that my father was making a name for himself, keeping up appearances was a critical aspect of his success.

Although my parents had to work hard for everything they had, success came quickly for them. In those days, building up name recognition and being the face of your business meant everything, especially in a city where there were only five or six restaurants and they were all named after their owners. I'd say that back then, he was like a celebrity in town, but he'd never put that in anyone's face. If someone on the street needed a dollar, he'd give them a dollar. He always treated everybody equally and was always very humble about his success. He took his role as a job provider very seriously, and he really cared about people. I remember sitting in my dad's restaurant one day when a man named Floyd came in looking for employment. He looked pretty rough around the edges, unshaven and malnourished. A lot of business owners would have turned a man like that away, based on appearances alone, but not my dad. Not only did he give him a job there on the spot, but he invited him to sit down and bought him lunch, probably the first real meal he'd had in a while. That was my dad. Whenever he could, he took that extra step to show people that he valued them. Even though he was a business man, he knew that life was about more than just dollars and cents.

My mother was a big presence too. She was an amazing singer; that was her claim to fame. I don't really remember her singing, but my uncles always talk about her gorgeous voice. On top of that she was a beautiful woman. I'll never forget when John F. Kennedy was campaigning for president, he came to Grand Rapids and the motorcade went right past my dad's restaurant. He actually looked twice at my mom, which was no surprise because, in addition to being a beauty, she looked a lot like Rose Kennedy. She would end up passing away in 1963, which was the same year that President Kennedy was assassinated.

Being in the restaurant business, you sacrifice for everybody. I'm not saying we were perfect – far from it – but my mother created a nice home for us. My parents chose to build a new house right next to the little place where we were currently living. It's such a shame, because she never got to live in it. We lost her too soon.

She picked out the design of the house from the architectural page of The Grand Rapids Press, and it was a dream of theirs to build that two-story home. I think it was important to her that each of us to have our own bedroom, because the other house was so small that all four of us kids shared one room. It's sad that she had to die at such a young age. The house hadn't been finished yet. It was right next door, so right up to her death she could look outside every day and see the progress of her dream home being built...a home that she would never get to live in.

My mom died from a blood clot a couple of weeks after giving birth to my sister, Liz. We still moved into the new house and sold the other one next door. Her design is still there. Her memories are still there. Of course, the house she brought us up in is still right next door and it's nice to see the little place where we got our start. I don't go in it, but I look at the outside and think about all of my parents' sacrifices and hard work, and how they helped shape the person that I am today.

I think I took some of my best traits from both of my parents.

I learned to be frugal from my dad — turning off lights, using one straw in a drink, giving one bar napkin instead of two, using a jigger to measure one ounce when you pour a shot of whiskey and never over-pouring. Those were the lessons of being concise in your business; every penny counts.

I think I have my mom's heart. Kindness and generosity always went hand-in-hand with her idea of running a business. In her role as a leader, she felt responsible for the well-being of their employees, and she treated everyone who worked at my dad's restaurant like they were an extension of our family.

I think that having both my dad's business sense and my mom's heart makes for a good mixture, and to be truly successful both professionally and personally you can't have one without the other.

It's the right mixture, especially in today's times, when a lot of business owners are thought of as being greedy and heartless and uncaring towards their employees. Certainly there are those out there who give business ownership a bad name, but I'd also like to speak on behalf of the millions of business owners, like myself, who know that no good company should be run without caring for its employees, the people who really make it possible for me to be where I am today.

The unfortunate stereotype of a greedy or heartless business owner is unfair a lot of times, and it's certainly not who I am. I don't enjoy firing people. I don't enjoy having to tell someone who comes in looking for work that I don't have a job for them. I see the way they lower their head, their shoulders slump, and the disappointment washes over their face. I don't enjoy that. I don't enjoy going to an unemployment hearing

when somebody has done something to get him or herself dismissed from a job. I don't enjoy writing someone up because I have to discipline them. I know that
as a business owner I have to do it, but I don't hire
people to fire them. My goal is to help them just as
much as they help me.

It's a corny, corny, corny phrase, but, yes, I consid-
er the people who work for me to be part of my family.
I've gone to their parents' funerals and to their daughters' weddings. I've seen some of their children grow
up in my place.

We had one kid, Jacob, whose parents both worked
for me, and the restaurant was his home away from
home. I remember his parents, George and Michelle,
would bring him to work with them and put the baby
carrier near the heat lamp, like an incubator. They'd
put him in front of the kitchen line when he was just a
baby while they did their work. I've seen Jacob grow
up to go to college. His mom, who has worked for me
for 24 years, is still here.

I've had second generations work for me. I had one
waitress who'd bring her daughter to the restaurant
and the little girl would hang on her mother's leg,
peaking out bashfully and then hiding her face again.
Now that same daughter is a waitress for me. That's
pretty cool.

When I think about my parents' humble beginnings, and the life I've led that's brought me to this
place, I know that what they taught me still holds
true: a restaurant is a family, and I couldn't have had
my success without understanding that I need to use
both my head and my heart.

Side Dish
A Very Special Order To Go

You never forget some of the special orders from customers.

The most special and unforgettable of them all was a simple take-out order from a somber-looking male in his late 20s whom Tommy Brann greeted at the door after entering his restaurant near lunchtime.

"It was about 11:30 a.m. and I had this guy come in and place a take-out order. He asked me, 'Well, what's your best steak?' I said, 'Our filet is our best steak.' It's eight ounces and it's the tenderest, leanest, best steak on the menu," Tommy Brann recalled. "So, he said he'd like to order the filet, and I told him he gets two sides with that. I asked him if he wanted a salad, baked potato, or fries.

"He told me, 'No, I just want the filet.' I explained to him it was no extra charge for the side items, but he still didn't want them. Then he told me, 'It's for my dog. It's his last meal. I have to put my dog down and I love him so much, I just want him to have the very best meal that he can possibly have.'

"Being a dog lover, I never forgot that."

It so touched Brann that he refused to charge the man for that steak.

"I bought the filet for him, so I told him that was from both of us to his dog. I'm glad his dog had a great last meal on Brann's. Maybe some people couldn't relate to it," Tommy Brann said, "but being a dog owner and a dog lover – dogs have been such a big part of my wife Sue's and my life for so long – it made perfect sense to me."

His love affair with man's best friend started four decades ago when he and Sue cared for a Labrador retriever owned by one of his former waitresses, Linda Kuzma, while she had taken a week of vacation.

"We took care of her dog, Max. He was a lot of fun," Tommy Brann said. "That's why Sue and I ended up getting a Lab after that. That's why it meant a lot to me to buy that filet for that guy and his dog.

"I was proud to buy that steak so that his dog could have a very special last meal."

"Your most unhappy customers are your greatest source of learning."
—*Bill Gates*

Chapter 4:
Customer Appreciation

At age 13, I'd hang around my father's restaurant and go in there for steaks and stuff. I wasn't working there 100 percent. I would go in there and do little odd jobs to help out my father. My dad never pressured us to become involved in the family restaurant. Instead, he had a different type of leadership.

You considered his stature as a local entrepreneur and small-business leader in the Grand Rapids community so much, you wanted to work for him. You have to push people sometimes, but, in my father's case, I think people looked at him as a leader and respected him for what he accomplished. He made a lasting impression on people, especially his customers, because he worked hard to meet and exceed their expectations.

It's another business lesson: Not letting people down.

"Profit" is such a powerful word in business, but, what I learned early on in the restaurant business is, if you came in with your girlfriend and I happened to give you a bad steak or dirty silverware, which I've done, that's my responsibility and I have to make it right. I don't like letting people down. I've done it and I'll do it in the future, and you've got to be tough, but you should never accept it.

I think following through is another important lesson.

Follow through and details are important. If you do let a customer down, if that person has a tough steak, for example, you first do whatever is necessary to correct that mistake for the customer and then you call your meat company to let them know about the poor quality of that particular piece of meat. If that happens, I'll give the customer another meal or a gift certificate to return for a better experience at my restaurant in the future. If a steak is overcooked, I'll talk to the cook about it. I actually have a note in my briefcase to talk to Jack, one of my cooks here, about overcooking a steak. Even though it's only one steak, it's important to me because it was a takeout order so I didn't get a chance to fix it right then and there. I make it a point to follow through, especially if a customer had a disappointing experience, and pay attention to all of the details.

I remember this lady in my restaurant, she had a complaint about her meal and she was from Texas. She had a legitimate complaint and I told her I was going to send her a gift card from Brann's to make up for it, but I lost her address. I know she probably thought I was just a talker. It happened about three or four years ago. I wish someday she'd call me on it because I don't like letting people down. I remember another time, I let a customer from Florida down, but I made up for it. She sent me an email and told me she didn't like this and she didn't like that. I knew that sending her a Brann's gift certificate wouldn't matter because she was from Florida, so I sent her a Chili's gift certificate. It was a $20 gift certificate. That's the way I do business.

It was a small gesture, but I wanted to make sure I followed through on it. Those things go hand-in-hand in terms of being a successful small-business owner. If it's their own business and their own money, people take care of their own money better.

What I've learned from being a small businessman is that I'm a good member in other businesses, civic organizations and other collaborations, because I treat the money like it's my own. So, if somebody comes to my place, and let's say they're working for $8 an hour at Walgreen's, if they get a bad steak, that's one hour of their hard work down the tubes because of me. I don't take that lightly. The restaurant business is unforgiving. I could go to Macy's and get a shirt, and if it has a button missing I just take it back and I'll still be a Macy's customer. If you serve one cold baked potato, you could easily lose a customer for life.

Free enterprise can be unforgiving. With the exception of a few giant corporations like General Motors and Chrysler, if you have a bad month, or a bad year, or couple of years, no one is going to come along and bail you out. Is that bad or good? I think it's probably good because it forces businesses to take responsibility. It forces them to do better if profits are low. You don't want to disappoint any of your customers. If that happens, ask yourself what you're prepared to do as a small-business owner to get it right.

I'm prepared to do whatever is takes to make it right for all of my customers.

I've learned that even the smallest details enhance the customer's experience at my restaurant, and following through on anything that doesn't meet a customer's expectations is essential to protecting my business.

I inherited those valuable lessons from my father, and I've never forgotten them.

Side Dish
Celebrity Sightings

Some restaurants put up walls of fame with signed pictures of celebrities.

The sports memorabilia hanging on the walls inside Tommy Brann's Steakhouse is partly a reflection of some of the larger-than-life athletic figures who have dined at his restaurant. The honor roll of famous people includes: four-time Super Bowl champion quarterback Terry Bradshaw of the Pittsburgh Steelers; NBA legend Larry Bird; former Detroit Lions running back Steve Owens; and the late Mark, "The Bird," Fidyrch, a former Detroit Tigers pitcher who became a national phenomenon by talking to the baseball, grooming the pitcher's mound and striking out batters at a stunning rate during the 1976 season.

The most famous diner, however, was boxing champion Sugar Ray Leonard.

"I think Sugar Ray Leonard was the most unique celebrity we ever had in the restaurant," Tommy Brann recalled. "First of all, he was famous like crazy. It was 20 years ago, when he was in his prime.

"Hills Department Store brought him in for an appearance. Hills used to bring in lots of celebrities, and its store in Grand Rapids wasn't located far from our restaurant, so, they'd bring them here after the appearances to eat," he said. "Sugar Ray Leonard came in and we had a 'Pac-Man' machine in the front lobby, so he sat down and started playing the game. My customers started coming in for lunch and they were stunned. They didn't bother him, but they looked at him and got their tables – and just kept looking at him."

Tommy Brann called his brother Mike to hustle down to the restaurant.

The thing he remembers most about Leonard's dining experience was the strange order he placed – or at least it seemed odd since the professional fighter was in the midst of his championship run.

"He's this big, tough fighter, so you would think he would order a big steak and a salad and maybe a draft beer or a shot of whiskey. Instead, he had a strawberry daiquiri and a breaded-shrimp dinner," Brann said.

"It's fine, but it's still a frou-frou drink and something that's fried," he added with a laugh. "If anything, it assured me of the guy's confidence in himself. I liked that a lot. We left him alone."

Everyone in the restaurant couldn't help but notice the champ.

"The customers knew who he was, but they were respectful, too. I was working during lunch hour anyhow," said Brann, who didn't make a spectacle of the situation, "so I didn't have time to gawk over him, either."

"I believe in God, family and McDonald's. And in the office, that order is reversed."
—Ray Kroc

Chapter 5:
Dreams and Nightmares

Before John Brann's steakhouse was even a pipe dream, my father opened a small business called the Stag Bar. It was located on Division Avenue and Oakes Street, two streets down from the house where he spent his childhood, and it was the collective dream of both he and his older brother, Tom.

It would later become their nightmare.

They both had traits that were valuable to their young business partnership. My dad wasn't an A student in school, but his common sense was unbeatable, and even though he was a younger brother, he was a leader of the family. He also had an entrepreneurial spirit. Although he was young when they came up with the idea for the Stag Bar, he had already run both a drug store and a parking lot. He was a natural leader, and he understood his market, an average blue-collar guy, because that's who he was.

Tom, for whom I was named, was a milk inspector. What I learned from him is that when he worked, he did it in a nice way. The power didn't go to his head. He did his job well, and the people whose places he inspected liked him. So, later on, when my uncle opened his own restaurant in the same building as the Stag Bar, his former customers became his current customers because they liked him. I've always kept that lesson with me throughout my career. Building good relationships with people promotes loyalty, and the better you treat the people you work with the more it benefits everyone in the long run.

I was still pretty young, of course, but I remember my dad telling me the story about getting started in the Stag Bar. His uncle George lent both he and my Uncle Tom the $5,000 they needed to open the business, and they built a working man's haven where you didn't have to break the bank to play some poker and get a good sandwich and a beer.

The Stag Bar was well-known for its 5-cent drafts and 10-cent shots of whiskey, as well as their corned beef sandwiches. My dad always bragged about their quality, and how they only used the best, Harding's corned beef from Chicago. He also took a lot of pride in the cleanliness of the restaurant. These days we take it for granted that our food is never handled without gloves, but at that time, when my dad insisted that they cut the corned beef with a knife and fork and then put it on the sandwich, it was a relatively new concept. He was really very powerful and innovative in his conviction that food shouldn't be touched by hands.

My dad let his health code ideals lapse slightly by making their signature bean soup at home, and then transporting it to the restaurant in a giant vat in the back of his car. He really took pride in making that soup. He soaked the ham and he soaked the beans and then cooked the soup himself; I'm talking a big, big, big tub of it. I'll never forget that soup. The smell of it always reminds me of riding to school in the morning, because it spilled in the trunk once and so the car carried that signature scent for a while. That soup was a big part of my childhood, and thanks to the strong link between the sense of smell and memory, I think it will be ingrained in my mind forever.

Simple as the operation was, the Stag Bar had done well. Sometimes it cashed $50,000 worth of business checks, railroad checks, in a single day, which was amazing. Unfortunately, with its success came problems for my dad and his brother.

Without really consulting my Dad, Uncle Tom took the money he'd earned from the Stag Bar and opened a steakhouse next door. He named it the Porterhouse Room, and featured what we call "big steaks," high end cuts, fine wines, and overall a fancy atmosphere that was in sharp contrast to what he and my dad were doing at the Stag. Uncle Tom's new venture did well, and before long he was looking to expand. Taking over the Stag Bar was the logical solution, but that meant that he would basically push my dad out of the business.

It wasn't rivalry. It was mainly my uncle wanting to expand his business, but to my dad it felt like a betrayal. When my uncle pushed him out he was like a man without a home. Needless to say, they parted ways on bad terms, and severed all ties both professional and personal. Their dream had turned into a nightmare, and what had been a close relationship and prospering partnership went down the tubes.

I think my dad enjoyed and preferred what he was doing at the Stag Bar. It was a nice, simple concept, and it was working. It doesn't work, however, when you get forced out by your own brother and you lose your relationship, as well as your way of making a living.

My dad responded by opening John Brann's Steakhouse on Burton and Division in Burton Heights.

It didn't mean it was an automatic success. As a small businessman, my father, who had a wife and four children, was suddenly putting everything on the line by opening his own restaurant. He didn't know if the place was going to make it or not. There were nights when I recall him telling me that the restaurant was doing less than 20 dinners. It was a difficult time for my parents. That's when my mother wrote that letter to my Uncle Al saying how much they were struggling. "Sorry I haven't been in touch lately. This is overwhelming. Say a prayer for us."

Side Dish
My Best Friend, Howie

One of the great pleasures in Tommy Brann's life is his love for dogs.

He gets up every morning and takes his 14-year-old mixed Lab, Howie, for a long walk. Naturally, Howie is always waiting by the door at the proper time and ready to share that bonding time with his best friend.

"He's getting up there in age," Brann said of his faithful companion. "Most of our dogs have been strays that people found. My sister found Howie and Casey abandoned in Byron Center and tied to a post. She brought them both to us.

"My wife, Sue, and I put an ad in the paper, but I'm glad nobody claimed them because we loved them both. We found Howie and Casey when they were puppies and it was such a shame that they had been tied up."

His affection for dogs has deepened through the years.

"Dogs are just loving. People, you have to work at loving them, but with dogs there's this unconditional love. It's a nice break from the restaurant business at times to be alone with Howie on those walks of ours," he explained. "The restaurant business is the toughest business in the world because you're dealing with so many variables all the time. It's a lot of stress, but there's no stress with Howie.

"I love coming home to my wife, Sue, and to our dogs. Howie is definitely man's best friend."

Admittedly, it wasn't love at first sight. In the early years of running his restaurant, Brann remained far too preoccupied with his business to tend to a pet. His brother, Joe, adopted his very first dog shortly after he opened Tommy Brann's Steakhouse on S. Division Avenue in Wyoming at the age of 19.

"I had one dog, Sizzler, who was named after the steak," he recalled. "I think someone gave him to me as a present, but I couldn't take care of him when I first started. Joe, thank God, took care of him because I was at the restaurant all the time."

It all changed when Tommy and Sue Brann did some dog-sitting for an employee.

A waitress, Linda Kuzma, entrusted the Branns with the care of her Lab. The couple became so smitten with that dog, they had to get a Lab of their own. It was the perfect addition to their household, one that has continued for several years.

His wife also had a mixed collie, Mary, when Brann met her.

Now, he looks forward to the walks with Howie just as much as his best friend does.

"I have been walking Howie a lot more this past year because I want to make up for lost time with him," he said. "So, I take him for a walk every morning. He's right there at the door waiting for me.

"I'm so glad I get to spend that time with him every morning."

During May of 2013, 14-year-old Howie suffered a life threatening incident in which his stomach turned over on itself, a somewhat common occurrence in older dogs. They took him to Michigan Vets on Fuller Street and Brann simply handed over his charge card, saying, "Do whatever it takes to save Howie."

Thankfully, Howie made it through the surgery, but during the frightening period while they were waiting for his surgery to be completed and didn't know if Howie was going to make it, Tommy posted on his Facebook wall about the tragic turn of events, just to vent.

Howie received over 400 likes and over 100 comments offering prayers and support. "It was a real comfort to know how many dog lovers there are out there who knew how Sue and I felt, not knowing whether Howie would live or die. When they took him back to his little cage after the surgery he was shivering. The staff was very caring and wrapped him in blankets, but I felt so sorry for my baby. It may sound a little out there, but Howie is part of our family and coming home to him wagging his tail after I've had a long day at work has made me feel like my life makes sense more than once."

"I feel that luck is preparation meeting opportunity."
—Oprah Winfrey

Chapter 6:
Origin of the Sizzler

After splitting up, my dad and his older brother didn't speak for a couple of years.

The Sizzling Steak, of all things, would be the thing that would help repair the relationship between them.

In terms of what happened to them over the Stag Bar, you could say it's not personal, it's just business, but my father had a family, and he took it personally.

I think this idea applies to business overall. You can say it isn't personal, but it is. You can't say it's just business. You can't tell me that when a customer complains, it isn't personal. You can't separate that. I was 10 years old when my dad and uncle severed ties, so I don't know all of what went on between them, but I know that it was hard for both of them, to say the least. Luckily, sometimes the most difficult experiences in life can teach you the most. But even in business, you can't learn from those trying times unless you take it somewhat personally.

Around the same time that my dad was opening his own restaurant, my Uncle Tom suffered the first of two heart attacks.

Of course, my dad and Uncle Tom hadn't been on speaking terms for a long time.

My aunt Millie, Tom's wife, came to my dad and said, "Please go see him. He's in the hospital," but he wouldn't go. I don't know if he was bitter, but my dad was still affected by my uncle's decision to open up the Porterhouse Room while forcing my dad out of the Stag Bar, the business they'd started together.

My dad finally did go to see him and they made up. Thank God for that.

During this time, before they made up, my dad opened John Brann's in Burton Heights, and my uncle was a mover and shaker in Grand Rapids too. Uncle Tom had gone to Chicago and he'd seen this steak and thought, "This would be good for my brother." It wasn't right for what he was doing at the Porterhouse Room, which was like Ruth's Chris Steakhouse back then. Expensive. Caviar. That was my uncle.

It was when he saw this smaller steak, which wouldn't be appropriate for the Porterhouse Room's menu, that he told my dad about it and brought it back to him. To my dad's credit, he then took it and developed it into the "Sizzler," put it on a serving plate, garlic butter over it, seasoned it, and sent it out sizzling.

That's the history of it right there.

It's sort of the good and the bad with my dad and his brother. My uncle did kick my dad out of the location for the Stag Bar, but then he came back and brought the "Sizzler" idea from his trips to Chicago. He didn't intend it to be a way to mend fences, but it shows that he couldn't think about business without thinking of my dad. Under all the hurt, that respect and similarity between them was still there. I think that's an important business lesson too: You should mind your own business, but be thinking about what other businesses are doing as well. When Tom was in Chicago, he wasn't just looking out for himself; he saw something that would work for my dad and he made that connection. It reminds me, too, of the way he treated his customers when he was a milk inspector. He did his job and did it well, but he was mindful of how to treat other people with respect while he did it...kind of a "what goes around comes around" way of doing things.

The relationship between my dad and his brother had been fractured for a long time, but ultimately they got back together after my uncle's heart attack and my dad had opened his restaurant. I remember after my mom died, my Uncle Tom would take us to dinner, the whole family. He picked us up at our house and took us to dad's place and bought dinner once a week. He was a big part of our lives and he was a great man.

I didn't fully grasp just how great he was until later. When my mom died, he and my Aunt Millie became part of the family again, and they cared and they knew how much it meant to us.

We had my mom's wake at Scotty's, which is an old restaurant on Division Avenue, and my uncle paid for it. He meant a lot to my dad. As far as the kids, we didn't know about their problems. We were pretty young at that time.

After they mended their relationship they had a fun kind of friendly rivalry. They would compare totals.

My dad had certain sayings, like, "a slow boat to China" if he had a really slow night or "it's a boomer" if he'd had a good night. They respected each other and they enjoyed being able to relate to one another as business owners in the same market, competing but rooting for each other at the same time.

My uncle's place in Grand Rapids, the Porterhouse Room, was known throughout the country.

You'd have famous people like Bonanza's sheriff, Ray Teal, coming in there. Milton Berle and a lot of celebrities would make it their place to eat when they came through town.

It was high-class, so it was THE place to go.

My dad's place was Applebee's before Applebee's was invented. It was a middle-class, affordably-priced restaurant that people could go to every day instead of just weekends or special occasions. My dad didn't even know he invented that, but he sure did. It was $1.95 at lunch hour for a Sizzler, and that included two sides. That's a pretty good price. It was $2.99 at night. We'll never lose that lesson from my dad. You have to be affordable for the people to come out to eat. It's part of free enterprise to set whatever price you want, but we wanted to make sure we never lost that lesson of making it easy for people to have a good meal in a great atmosphere. Of course we have to turn a profit, but we don't want to charge more than we need to.

Uncle Tom died at age 65 following a second heart attack. He died at home. My dad ended up helping my aunt with the Porterhouse Room after that. I chipped in by doing the bookwork in the morning.

At his funeral they had 300 people sign the book and we had a police escort that went down Division Avenue. I still remember a man taking his hat off in respect for my uncle.

He was really well-respected in Grand Rapids. Unfortunately, the Porterhouse Room didn't last long because my aunt, well, she wanted to do it herself. I love my Aunt Millie, but it was too much for her to take on. It's another important lesson: Every day, you have to stay on top of your small business.

Subsequently, the Porterhouse Room failed, even though it was a long-established name.

Regardless of how it ended, Uncle Tom made his mark both on the industry and on our family, and that will never change. For me, the Brann's Sizzling Steak will always represent both my father's legacy as a restaurant owner and his reconciliation with my Uncle Tom. It's another way that the restaurant and family go hand-in-hand for us. Business broke them up and business brought them back together.

Side Dish
Some Things Never Go Out of Style

The Sizzling Steak has been the No. 1 menu item forever.

It was the signature dish upon which family patri-
arch John Brann Sr. founded his original steakhouse
in Burton Heights in 1961 and the mouth-watering
sirloin covered in garlic butter and served on a sizzling
plate remains the top-selling item on the menu at
Brann's locations more than four decades later.

In that time, the Sizzling Steak has undergone
some subtle changes.

"We've made some very small changes to the Sizzling Steak," Tommy Brann said. "It's still served on a
sizzling platter with garlic butter. My dad introduced
the garlic butter in 1961 and that's a big part of it. I
don't think that'll ever change. You now can get different sauces over the steak – a bourbon sauce, our
own version with a Boursin cheese sauce, a shrimp
sauce with little pieces of shrimp, and we recently
added a lobster sauce. I'm proud that we've taken such
an iconic steak and kept it pretty much the same

through the years and allowed people to add their favorite sauces to it.

"It's one of my proudest things about our restaurants."

In four-plus decades of the Sizzling Steak, the Brann's chain has made very few changes in its meat supplier.

The original meat supplier, Pastoor Brothers, a Grand Rapids outfit, had an exclusive contract for many years until the owner retired and closed the business. In all, there have been just four meat suppliers.

"Pastoor Brothers made my dad's meat for many years, very loyal, but then they retired. It wasn't a management decision or anything like that," Brann recalled. "For years, they were the ones I always made my check out to. I'll never forget when they left the business; they gave me my last check back.

"I had always paid my meat bill ahead of time. They gave me that final check back with interest."

A supplier out of Ada, Ryskamp's, was next, followed by Superior Meat Company.

The Sizzling Steak supplier for the past decade has been Davis Creek Meat in Portage.

"Something as important as that, you just don't switch every week," Brann said of making sure to protect the Sizzling Steak legacy. "It's very important to have stability there, just like with my servers and my employees who've been with me for 30 years or more. It always has been our signature product.

"I go back to the Beatles. Paul McCartney still has his original bass guitar. You'll see him onstage with it. Some of that is because of nostalgia, but it's also because it's a great bass guitar," he added. "I would compare our Sizzler to that – you don't want to switch the meat supplier too often. You want to keep the changes to a minimum."

The 8-ounce portion size has remained a constant during that time.

In addition, Brann's has introduced a 6-ounce petite cut and a 12-ounce version for heartier appetites.

"We used to have just an 8-ounce Sizzler. Now, we also have a smaller Sizzler and a bigger Sizzler. It's still essentially the same Sizzling Steak my dad introduced in 1961. We haven't changed it much, which is a good decision," Brann said.

"It is still the No. 1 menu item and it always has been the No. 1 menu item."

It even became the top-selling menu item when Brann's opened a pair of locations in the metropolitan Detroit area, where the Sizzling Steak had no legacy like it did on the west side of the state.

It was a unanimous favorite of Detroit-area diners right from the start.

"Even when we opened the place in Northville eight years ago, the Sizzling Steak became our No. 1 seller immediately," Brann said. "People there didn't even know what it was. We didn't know what to think, but that just proves how popular the Sizzling Steak was all those years and how popular it still remains."

"Far and away the best prize that life offers is the chance to work hard at work worth doing."
—Theodore Roosevelt

Chapter 7:
The Legend of Dorothy Clark

I was on the way up in my dad's restaurant at age 17.

I had learned a lot about running a small business by getting my hands dirty and doing almost every possible job in his restaurant. Cooking was my next accomplishment, and this is where I learned another important lesson.

Dorothy Clark was the broiler cook for my father.

At that time, she would prepare more than 800 steaks on a Saturday, which was an impressive number. There were only about seven Grand Rapids-area restaurants in those days: Duck's; Sayfee's; the Porterhouse Room, owned and operated by my Uncle Tom; Scotty's; Duba's; Hatten's; and John Brann's Steakhouse.

My dad fully developed this great concept of the Sizzler steak – an 8-ounce bottom sirloin served on a sizzling-hot platter with garlic butter over it. He had the foresight to position and market it as an affordable blue-collar steak, which attracted people to his restaurant during the week instead of only on the weekend. As I've mentioned, the Sizzling Steak was Brann's signature dish, and its preparation is what made Dorothy so valuable to my father's restaurant.

Her ability to meet the enormous demand for the Sizzling Steak made her not only an indispensable asset to my dad's restaurant, but also a key part of our family; my dad knew the talent of Dorothy Clark. On Saturday night, she would cook 800 Sizzlers herself. She'd stand over that grill and turn them out, never sacrificing quality for speed. She was amazing. At the end of the night, she'd come to the bar and my dad would say, "How many did we do?" She'd say, "Well, we did around 1,000 dinners." Those would be about 800 steaks and 200 other dinners.

Every Saturday night, she'd get a fifth of vodka from my dad, which was a little bonus.

My dad thought so much of Dorothy that he bought her a house. She deserved it. She hardly ever missed work, but one Saturday she was really sick and couldn't come in. So, like a football team losing a valuable player, my father was wondering how we would make it through such a busy night.

My dad decided to make a desperate attempt to replace Dorothy for the night with not one, but two cooks, an employee named Willie, and me. Now, Willie was a good cook, but he wasn't real fast. I was just 17 years old and still learning that sometimes in small business you have to go with the flow and make the best of the challenges that come your way. I was a newbie behind the grill and filling the shoes of our head chef was a daunting task. Having us double-team it was a really smart move on my dad's part because we made a good duo; where one of us fell short the other was there to pick up the slack.

So, Willie and I were pushed into action, and together we did what neither of us could have done alone. We did about 800 steaks that night. It took two guys to take Dorothy's place, but we did it.

I think the valuable lesson there was to go with the flow. I've had toilets overflow on Mother's Day, which is the busiest day of the year for us. I've had burners go out during the dinner rush. I've had line cooks walk out on their shift and bartenders not show up. In those times, when it seems like anything that could go wrong will go wrong, you have to take a deep breath and deal with it as best you can. Ultimately things always seem to turn out OK at the end of the day.

My dad was the king of going with the flow. He did it that one night when Willie and I had to cook 800 Sizzlers. Even though it took two people to replace Dorothy, small business and John Brann's Steakhouse survived to fight another day. I enjoyed being busy and I enjoyed helping my dad out of a bad situation. I liked working hard and sweating back then, and I still like it.

Dorothy Clark worked for my dad at his place until it closed.

The other lesson there is that small business is not all about profit; it's about people, too. Just as Dorothy Clark was an integral part of my dad's business,

Frank Van Norman was an important part of my restaurant and my life. They shared many of the same qualities. They were both hard, honest workers, and Frank was someone I could always rely on. I truly felt that my business wouldn't be the same without him, and he was my friend too. Once again, I've found that people like Frank and Dorothy prove that in small business you can't completely separate the personal from the professional. Their dedication and effort every day made them part of the family.

They inspired me so much that I eventually formed a scholarship fund at Grand Rapids Community College for African-American students. It was my small way of trying to provide others with the same opportunities for success that I was afforded, as well as the type of support and dedication I was given by people like Frank.

I'll never forget how in that one night I gained a special appreciation for Dorothy Clark and her importance to my father's restaurant. She was well-liked, good at her job, and represented my father in a way that made us all proud.

Side Dish

Tribute to "Big Rick" the Bartender

Every restaurant has some unforgettable personalities on its staff.

One of the most memorable at Tommy Brann's Steakhouse was "Big Rick" DeVries the bartender. You couldn't miss him. He was a large man with an equally impressive personality, Tommy Brann recalled.

"He was like a celebrity in town. He started as a dishwasher for me. He was 400 pounds, he graduated from Godwin Heights and he started working for me right out of high school," Brann said. "He was a high school wrestler and very athletic, but he was big. He was about 6 foot, but he was a lot more wide than tall."

His unique character made him a popular figure with customers.

"I made him a bartender 35 years ago, but he earned it. You start at the bottom in this business, like I did, and you work your way up. He was a dishwasher, but when he got back there behind the bar he was fast and he became a celebrity," Brann said. "He had his own little following. He worked for me for more than 20 years. I remember he bought a house right down the street from the restaurant. Sadly, he died at his house. He was in his early 40s, but he had some leg problems and he had congestive heart failure."

Big Rick is gone, but he hasn't been forgotten.

"I was good for Big Rick and he was good for me. He was a big part of my life and I was a big part of his life," Brann said of his famed bartender. "I know that Big Rick really enjoyed his job here."

*"All our dreams can come true –
if we have the courage to pursue them."*
—Walt Disney

Chapter 8:
On My Own

I never questioned whether I would follow in my father's footsteps.

When I was younger I'd thought about being a police officer, but as I got older it seemed natural to follow my dad and be a restaurateur. He was going to send me to Ferris State College. I even went up to Big Rapids with a friend, Rick, and looked around the campus.

I was pretty set on the school but in the meantime, while I worked for my dad, I began to get more and more immersed in the world of small business. I was just a high school kid working hard to help out my dad, but somewhere in there it turned into something more. Without really realizing it I was learning how to run a restaurant.

First and foremost, I wanted to please my dad, so I did it the way he did it. I watched and learned from him after he purchased the Par 4 restaurant and started over again with John Brann's Steakhouse in Burton Heights following the split with my Uncle Tom over the Stag Bar. It was also really important to me that I didn't come off like a spoiled kid, mooching off of my dad's success, so I tried to work harder than anyone to show that I didn't feel entitled to inheriting what my father had built, and I even worked off the clock a lot of the time. I don't think any of my father's customers or his employees ever questioned my work ethic, but I couldn't help but to care what people thought of me in that regard, and I put pressure on myself to prove my worth.

Of course, my dad's success didn't come right away. It was tough going at first. He sank all of his money into the new restaurant to compete in the free market. Like a gambler in a poker game, he knew the odds he was up against, but he had faith in the free enterprise system in America, and he felt like the wager was worth the risk.

One night, after a very slow start, my dad left and went home early. In small business, I've learned that you live and die with your business on a nightly basis. On that particular night, my dad was dying a little.

He got a phone call later that same night from a waitress who told him, "John, we sold 27 Sizzlers." Sales had picked up. It shows you that in my dad's restaurant his employees felt like they were on the same team as him. She made that phone call to brighten his day, and those little gestures mean a lot.

After learning how to cook I moved to bartending, and that is where I really excelled.

I was just plain fast, and my customers liked watching me tend bar. I was always especially conscious of my dad's liquor costs, and I would pour those shots accurately. We served Tom Collins, Harvey Wallbangers, Manhattans and, of course, bottled beer. Perhaps even more valuable than learning how to make drinks was the confidence that I developed from being behind the bar. Meeting so many new people made me less shy and opened my eyes to the world a little bit.

I learned a lot more about some of our customers than I ever imagined I would. People really open up to bartenders sometimes. You're like an unofficial therapist or confidant.

It was interesting to see how some of our customers led their lives, but I also learned as I got older not to judge my customers based on what I witnessed, because what happened on the other side of my bar is only one side of who those people are. I encountered a lot of married customers who ended up dating a lot of my dad's waitresses and as an 18-year-old working behind the bar I wasn't quite sure how to reconcile that. I liked my customers, and yet I disagreed with the choices they made at times.

I often tended bar during the lunch period, which was usually much busier than dinner and, of course, much faster-paced. At 11am we'd have 20 glasses with Bloody Mary mix in them ready to pour vodka, expecting those mid-day drink orders to come streaming in faster than I could pour them. This was 1968, and at that time it was fairly common for some customers to come in for lunch, have a few martinis, and then move to the bar for more drinks, never returning to work. I took all of this in and vowed I would never do that if I ever owned my own business. All of those lessons would follow with me when I started my small-business dream.

The opportunity to branch out on my own presented itself when The Southern Restaurant became available in 1971.

My dad recognized my work ethic and I knew I could run my own place. The Southern was owned by Pete Vrano, but it wasn't succeeding. Pete had owned a great business at the Cottage Bar in Grand Rapids, but he wanted a restaurant that was larger and a little classier so he bought The Southern at 4157 S. Division Ave. in Wyoming. When it didn't do well, Pete ended up selling The Southern to my dad and me, and my dad lent me $30,000 for the down payment. He did this instead of helping pay for my college education.

Instead of going to Ferris for restaurant management school as I had planned, I decided to make a straight line for business ownership. After all of my experience working in restaurants and a lifetime of watching my dad succeed as a business owner, studying how to do those same things in college seemed like an unnecessary extra step. My dad never tried to talk me out of going to school or convince me to follow in his footsteps; it was a choice that seemed natural and right to me. While other kids from high school were heading off to college or going to work for someone else, I opened my own restaurant; at the young age of 19 I started something that would last a lifetime.

Committing to that long-term goal was no casual decision. I knew from watching my dad that opening my small business meant an end to any normal life. As a small business owner, you have to be willing to take risks, but you should never base your decisions on emotion alone. I can't stress enough the value of having a non-biased adviser or accountant or friend whom you respect to help guide that choice. If you base a business decision purely on emotion, you're headed for a letdown.

Ultimately, my dad took the money he was going to give me for college and set up a payment plan with interest on the $30,000 he lent me to purchase The Southern and open my own place. It was the best thing he could have done for me because it made me feel like it was up to me to succeed or fail, just like he had done when he risked it all by opening up his steakhouse. For the first time in my life I felt independent and whole as a person.

It wasn't charity though; my dad made me pay back every penny. I was now an independent businessman and still leaning on my father a little, but not too much. Forty-two years later I can still hold my head high because I returned that money and made my own way after that, free and clear.

The last thing he did before sending me out on my own was to name my new place. He found an advertisement in the Detroit Free Press for Tommy Dove Restaurant and he liked the flow of "Tommy Dove." Thus, it was Tommy, not Tom, and on July 5, 1971, I began my first day at Tommy Brann's Steakhouse.

The first day we opened we did 97 dinners. I'm still there more than 42 years later.

In small business, I learned it's important to have a mentor. You'll have lots of them, in fact. Some of them you will know. Some of them you won't know personally, but you will learn from them. My dad was my first mentor, but he always encouraged me to have other mentors in my life too. He knew that I had other people who I looked to for guidance, including Amway Corp. co-founder Rich DeVos, whom I always looked up to because he was a self-made businessman from Grand Rapids.

Although I earned what I have, I couldn't have done it without my dad. I remember when he died; we went to Blodgett Hospital in East Grand Rapids. He was 90 years old and had succumbed to pneumonia. After we left the hospital, we went back to my dad's place where I came across some notes about customers and how he had remembered their names.

I was very impressed by how he made notes, how he followed through with the smallest details and just being personal. That's a lesson that has stuck with me for more than 42 years at my own place. Even after he was gone he was still teaching me.

Side Dish
Fistfights and Flashers

Every bar owner has some unforgettable stories to tell.

Such is the case for Tommy Brann, who, like it or not, has been involved in breaking up a handful of skirmishes involving bar patrons throughout the course of a proud 42-year restaurant career.

One such incident stands out from all the rest of them.

"It's part of owning a bar and dealing with people who drink alcohol. Sometimes, there's drama," Brann said of the occasional problem customer. "I remember it was summertime, it's about 2:30 in the morning and there's this guy outside in the parking lot with a draft beer. First of all, he's out there with my beer and he's breaking the law. He can get in trouble. Second of all, he's not supposed to have it because we're closed.

"So, I went outside and said, 'You can't have that' and 'give it back to me.'"

You can pretty much guess what happens next.

"You know, sometimes you can go with the flow, but sometimes you have to say enough is enough. He was going to finish drinking the beer, but, to me, that was disrespectful, and so, as I was going to grab it out of his hand, he hits me in the head with the glass mug. I lost it when he hit me over the head," Brann recalled.

Instinctively, Brann reacted and dropped his assailant.

"My adrenaline got going and I got him on the ground. Blood was coming from both sides of his mouth. I didn't care because it was self-defense," he said. "I went to the hospital and I had to get nine stitches in my head. I never knew they could give you shots in the head. I never knew they could do that, but they numb it right up and give you a shot right in the head. It wasn't that bad, it really wasn't."

His adrenaline kept pumping long after he had gotten stitched up.

"After I got home that night, I was still stoked. It was a good night for me. I think he got the worst of it because he left," Brann said with a hint of pride. "I didn't pursue it with the police. We have a nice bar here, but I've been involved in a few bar fights. It's part of being a small-business owner."

He also pointed out another memorable incident involving a belligerent customer.

"I remember one time our bartender, Big Rick, cut this girl off who had had too much to drink, and she got mad at him. The way she punished Big Rick is she took her shirt off and flashed him," Brann said. "I remember Rick saying, 'What kind of punishment was that?' Hey, I have survived them all."

Future restaurant people.
Little did we know the sacrifice it takes
to own a small business.
And to top that, the business is a restaurant.
—Tommy Brann

My dad, John Brann (l) and my uncle, Tom Brann. (r)

My Uncle Tom (l) and my dad (r) at the Stag Bar.

My mom, Liz Brann.
Candidate John F. Kennedy looked twice at my mom during
a motorcade on Division Ave.

Uncle Al Nicolette, my mom, my dad, and me.

Don Savage (l). He used to flick beer in my face when I was a kid.

My dad and Tom Brann at the Stag Bar.

John Brann and Jimmy Stratton

Menu cover

My dad's baseball team.

My family celebrating a birthday.

My dad's 70th birthday party.
From left: Tommy, Joe, Liz, John, Johnny, Mike.

Mayor Logie of Grand Rapids proclaimed September 7, 2001
John Brann Day.
From left: Joe, Tommy, John, Johnny, Liz, Mike

State Representative Tom Mathieu and John Brann.

My dad loved Thunderbirds.

My dad
The sharpest dresser in town.

My dad in front of his restaurant.

My dad's funeral.
Each car dropped a flower in front of his restaurant.

Me with my not-yet-wife, Sue, at her college graduation.

My beautiful wife, Sue, on our honeymoon in Hawaii.

My mom's brother, Uncle Ted, and Aunt Ellie.
I miss him a lot.

In front of my good friend John Gruner's place.
Sue, Tommy, Nancy with baby Kelly, and Mike

My wife, Sue, and my father-in-law, Cubby.

Mind Your Own Business radio show.

At the Free Enterprise Rally.

Supporters at the Free Enterprise Rally.

A twenty-one-gun salute.

My first salute.
Lt. Groendyke (l), Pvt. Brann (r)

Jake (l) and Millie (r)
A great part of my life; I miss them.

In front of The Whitehouse.

Brann's Sizzlin' Five
From left: Tom Doyle, Johnny Brann, Mike Brann, Tommy Brann,
Dave Lahay

Minding my own business and taking care of my baby.

"Your time is limited, so don't waste it living someone else's life."
—Steve Jobs

Chapter 9:
Different Legacies

I don't remember much about that first day at Tommy Brann's Steakhouse.

It was a blur.

I was living in a house on the property, which was part of the purchase of the restaurant. I had about a 50-yard walk across the parking lot from the front door of my house to the restaurant. Right from the beginning my work and my personal life were pretty much one and the same, or rather my work became my life. There's really no other way to do it if you want your business, your baby, to succeed. I was like a new father; I changed my life to center around this fragile, fledgling business that I had created. I do remember that first day — July 5, 1971 — went by fast. I had to be right back up the next morning to do it all over again.

I was confident, though, ready to dig in and do whatever it would take. I weighed 145 pounds back then. My dad was worried about me because I worked so hard. At that time in my life I didn't know about eating right, and it was just work, work, work. Once I got there, I started working. I didn't eat three squares because I was 19 years old and I was so busy with my restaurant. I ate a little here and there throughout the day but it basically wasn't important to me at that point.

I was behind the bar that first day. I got that from my dad; that's how he ran his place — from behind the bar. I've learned since then that things change and you've got to do things differently now, but I was a really good bartender. I was fast. I probably couldn't bartend worth beans right now, though, because I have to be involved in the entire operation. I wasn't tired after that first day of being open; instead I went home with a feeling of deep satisfaction. I like getting things done. I like that sense of accomplishment. As I said, it was a real blur, but it felt great.

I remember before I even opened, my dad, who really understood the importance of having good public relations, told me to put a bottle of whiskey on the bar and if anyone comes in during the remodeling, give them a drink. No charge. I had some people pop in from the neighborhood, just wondering what was going on and if we were open. So, I'd make them a little Manhattan cocktail and they'd look around and I'd talk to them. It was a really positive thing. I know we probably broke all sorts of laws doing that, giving them free drinks, but let's face it, things were differ-ent back then, and my dad's suggestion created a lot of good word-of-mouth before the opening of my place. We had torn the previous bar down. Any time you open up a new business you have to make changes, otherwise you're rubber-stamping the last regime and maybe you're in that place because the last regime didn't make it. If the former business wasn't success-ful, you need to signal to your customers that your place will be different, and one way to do that is by changing the aesthetics. All of that goes into creating an atmosphere, a special vibe that sets you apart from other places. Even in my early beginnings I think I knew that I would someday own more than one loca-tion, and I wanted to create a signature look and feel to the place that people would recognize no matter which Tommy Brann's they were in.

When we opened our doors we were still in the pro-cess of remodeling. Things were torn up pretty badly. The previous owner had a dance floor in there, so we took that out. It also had a U-shaped bar and we took that down, because it took up too much space in the dining room. We redid the bar and we redid the dining room. We installed red carpeting and red booths, be-cause that's what you did back then. We painted and refinished and made it all brand new.

I remember we also put some lights around the building. We had yellow, red, green — different-colored rainbow lights all around the place. I also re-member a lot of those lights disappearing. Some peo-ple stole them. They'd unscrew them and take them. It's something you'd never expect people to do but be-cause the lights were in the ground I guess people thought they were fair game, so that was the last time I ever put anything on the ground. That's how you grow in this business. It's trial and error and you'll make mistakes, but the important thing is that you change and adapt to the challenges that get thrown at you.

It's also good to know what things you should hold on to and never change. We kept the brick exterior of the building. It's still the same brick after more than 42 years. I told my wife, Sue, I want one of those bricks placed in my casket when I die. I want to take that with me. That'll be part of my legacy.

One thing I'll never forget from that first day was Carl Story coming into my restaurant. He was the owner of the biggest Oldsmobile dealership in the world at that time. He had a car dealership in Lansing and he had been a long-time customer at my dad's restaurant, and he stopped into my place that first night.

He bought the whole restaurant a drink. We weren't packed, but we had about 60 people in there. I have never had anybody do that since. I've had people who've bought the bar a drink, but not the entire restaurant. It was a great show of faith. In that one gesture he expressed his support of my new business venture and I'll never forget it.

I also remember he told me something that really helped my business and was an important lesson for me. He said, "I see some cigarette butts out front near the entrance. You have to keep those swept up. Those things matter." Now, here's a guy who owns the biggest Oldsmobile dealership in the world, and I'm thinking to myself that these are the sorts of little details that helped make him successful.

I thought it was pretty cool what Carl Story did, buying the whole restaurant a round of drinks and pointing out a small detail like keeping the entrance to my place looking nice and clean at all times. It's important to not be too prideful as a business owner. You have to trust in your own ideas but also be open to taking advice from others who have proven their success. No matter how small or unimportant it may seem, those little touches come together to make for a professional and inviting atmosphere that people want to return to.

To my credit, I took that advice to heart. I wasn't some cocky kid who didn't want someone else telling me how to run my business. I know today's generation might make a smart-ass remark back to him, but, no, I listened to him. I still think about Carl sometimes when I sweep up in my parking lot. I think about his comments, about the appearance of my place, and the lesson that he taught me. It makes me smile.

As stressful as it felt at times to be losing money by being closed during our initial remodeling, there was ten times more pressure when we finally opened for business. I know that might sound backward, but the days when you come in and your only worries are organizing your stockroom and cleaning your floors are the easy times; it isn't truly stressful until you open those doors and have to produce for your first customers. There's not much reason to be stressed until that happens.

Even after watching my dad for years, nothing could have prepared me for those first months of being the new owner of Tommy Brann's and knowing that everything was riding on my shoulders. I had to make sure that my employees were happy, my customers were happy, and of course I had the $30,000 loan from my dad to pay back. There was no one else to blame if things went south. I was the man in charge, and that was both a source of pride and a source of stress, and still is to a certain extent. When things go well you can pat yourself on the back, and when something goes wrong you know it's on you to fix it. It's no reason to be scared, though. You have to be prepared to perform.

So, looking back, I was 19 years old, working relentlessly from 8 a.m. until 2 a.m. Every day. Open to close. I had $5,000 payments that had to be made every month. My only focus was working, working, working. If I did not have that distraction of work and had to concentrate on the bills, I would have been flipping out.

Yet, it never fazed me. I even saved ahead and paid my meat bills before they were due.

That's not to say I didn't have a little paranoia at times. Being a little bit obsessive about your overhead and profit margin is good for a small-business person. If you are a little bit paranoid, you are less likely to lose your way or take things for granted. You don't want to drive yourself crazy with worrying about money, but if you never think about it you're headed down a bad path.

To this day, I still have a little bit of that paranoia in me. As a business owner it's hard to get out of the train of thought of saving money, even to be extravagant with giving a gift to the person you care about. Sometimes I'd want to buy something special for someone I loved but my business side struggled with making the purchase and generally won out. Bad or good, that's just the way it is. It's a balance between generosity and frugality, of enjoying the fruits of your labor and sharing it with others, but also not getting too comfortable, because the industry is unpredictable and you have to stay sharp.

My father's death brought this trait to the surface and, on top of grieving the loss of my dad, I found myself confronted with the challenge of reconciling the businessman in me with the family man I am as well.

At the age of 90, my dad was dying. I remember all of us, all of his children, were there in the hospital with him. At one point I asked my family to step out of the room so I could talk to my father face-to-face one last time.

I asked my dad to forgive me for not visiting him more often because my business had taken over my life. If anyone understood that, I know that my father did. He put his arm up and he hugged me.

As the eldest child in the family, I was the executor of my dad's estate. Although my dad was very wise, he was not wealthy. That's fine. In the free enterprise system, success is often measured by the size of your bank account. To my dad, success was measured by the number of people who attended a person's funeral, and, based on that, my dad definitely touched a lot of lives and was a great success. He had a packed church for his funeral.

I helped him get his affairs in order before he passed. He had a will, and I felt I had a firm sense of what his thoughts and wishes were.

I had been established in my own restaurant for several years at this point, and my business sense took over at the funeral home.

Picking out a casket is like buying a car. You can buy a Rolls Royce or you can get a Chevy Impala. There's a wide range of options. It's a much more emotional decision than buying a car, though. As the leader, I had a responsibility to look out for the others in the family, their inheritance, and making sure my dad's wishes were fulfilled.

I was very leery of buying a really expensive casket. That led to ... not a squabble, but a family discussion. The price difference between the caskets we were considering was several thousand dollars.

If you've ever had to price caskets for a departed loved one, you know they come in a variety of options and none of them are cheap. So, we were looking at caskets for dad, but the businessman in me was looking at the price. Although my brothers and sister disagreed with me, I think dad would have thought I was making the right choices. Even in that situation which was charged with emotion, I approached it purely as a business decision, which is something that I partly learned from my dad. My brothers and sister selected one casket that was more expensive than the one I thought we needed. In the end, however, I gave in to their choice in order to spare the family a fight at that delicate time, but my small-business mindset never wavered.

Even though we ended up getting the more expensive casket, I didn't see the price of the casket as being an acknowledgment of what my father had done in his life. To me, it was more about the packed Saint Thomas the Apostle Church in Grand Rapids and what we did to honor him at the end of his life when the funeral procession passed his restaurant. Each car in the procession was given a flower from the floral arrangements at the funeral home, and we had blocked off two parking meters in front of John Brann's Steakhouse on South Division.

As we processed from the church to the cemetery, we passed my dad's restaurant and every car slowed down and tossed the flower on the sidewalk in front of his place as a final goodbye. It was the only way we could have bid that final farewell to him because his restaurant had been a huge part of a lot of people's lives and a huge part of supporting his own family.

A lot of people remembered him and there were whole families who packed both the funeral home and the church. At 90 years old, most of your friends, sorry to say, probably have died, but my dad had a full church because there were generations of families who showed up to pay their respects to him. His influence had a trickle-down effect; it radiated out from everyone he touched and went way beyond what he probably even knew. It was like a presidential funeral, because we lost someone that was a big part of so many people's lives, some who had never even met him but were touched by his warmth and generosity. So many people felt like they wanted to be close to him in order to say farewell. It was a great goodbye to a great man.

I learned through the handling of my father's affairs after he died that it's not wrong to have a business mentality when making important decisions, but it's all right for personal feelings to be part of that process as well.

There is a fine line between family stuff and business. I don't think making that decision meant I loved my dad any less. In fact, in my mind, it meant I loved him just as much because I think that choosing a less expensive casket is what my dad would've done and what he would've wanted. I know he would have backed me up on my decision to go with a casket that was less expensive, but, when my sister, Liz, started crying, I also think my dad would've said, "Tom, this is not what I want for my family in the last few days of saying goodbye to me. I don't want my daughter crying." I heard that voice instead of the business voice. It's important to be open to decisions that may not seem completely practical, because sometimes they're the right thing to do anyway. Even in business, at the end of the day you're dealing with people, and human emotions are not always a rational matter, but they are very important.

My dad deserved the best, no doubt. I was just trying to think of the big picture, and the inheritance, and making sure his wishes were fulfilled. Some people that he cared about outside of the family and who he felt needed help got the inheritance. I wasn't getting the money. I didn't get anything from him. I had my own restaurant, I didn't need anything. In that sense I felt that it was up to me to make a wise business decision for the good of others involved. Like so many other instances in my life, I had to find a way to balance the personal and the professional in order to make the right choice. I also remembered to take the advice of a person who I trusted in making those choices. In this case, that guidance came from my father, not directly, but because I knew him so well I knew what he would have told me to do and I listened to that.

My dad didn't die a rich man, but I had already received my inheritance before his death. He gave me all that experience in the restaurant business and helped me get started in my own place. I'm eternally grateful to my dad for that. That was what he left me and it was priceless.

Side Dish
The Kindness of Brann's Aid

The partners at Brann's go the extra mile for some of their people.

Management accepts pleas for help and nominations from employees when severe hardship cases arise. If there is a special need that a paycheck just doesn't meet, employees can seek assistance.

"I got this idea a little bit from George Harrison and his concerts for Bangladesh for humanitarian relief and 'Farm Aid.' If we're doing good, we like to help our people out," Tommy Brann said.

"It's a special program just for employees and it has worked out really well."

Brann's Aid, which is submitted for approval at board meetings, has helped pay for funeral expenses, medical treatments, transportation and even purchased a furnace for a mother and children in the middle of winter.

"We had an employee who lost his father and couldn't afford to bury his dad. We had an employee with a blood disease who had to miss work. We've helped some of them with money to help pay their rent. We've even helped people who needed a car because they couldn't get back and forth to work," he said.

"All of this stuff we do for employees only, they don't have to pay it back."

Tommy Brann estimated 50 employees from different Brann's locations have benefitted from the program.

"It has to come in front of the board. We don't do this for someone who wants a vacation in Jamaica," he said. "Our employees are such good people they don't really take advantage of it as far as just saying, 'Oh, wow, I need $100, I'm going to make something up.' When people are in need, they're honest about it.

"A lot of times our employees don't even know that they've been nominated. It's people helping each other out. We're the trustees of it. It's been a great thing for us. The word 'business' is not a cold word."

Some recent examples were particularly heartwarming.

"We just did one for someone with a blood disease who couldn't afford treatment. We helped someone whose father got burned out of his apartment. I remember we bought a furnace for $750 for an employee whose family was cold in the winter time," he said. "We had to make a fast decision on that one.

"So, no questions asked, we bought a furnace for her and her kids."

Simple acts of kindness. No questions asked. Simple as that.

"Drive thy business or it will drive thee."
—*Benjamin Franklin*

Chapter 10:
Protecting the Baby

You need to treat your small business like a baby. It must get lots and lots of attention. It must be nurtured. It must not be ignored.

My small, 7,200-square-foot building cannot stick up for itself. It cannot stop a politician from taxing it. It cannot stop an attorney from suing it. It cannot stop a customer from damaging it. It cannot stop an employee from stealing from it. It cannot stop a city from closing the street in front of it for repairs.

That's my job – protecting my baby.

Naturally, there are times that test your patience. It happens to all of us.

It seems strange how things often seem to go wrong at my place on Christmas Eve. I once had three people walk out on a check of $128 one Christmas Eve, but I remembered those people. There was one big guy with a beard, another guy, and a lady. I said to myself when they first came in, "There's something different about them." I went out to them and talked to them for a little bit and said, "Hi." I got to talking to them about what motel they were staying at, which was right down the street from my place.

So, anyway, at 9 o'clock, (we close early on Christmas Eve anyway) my waitress came to me and said, "Those people walked out on me." I called the police and the police said they were too busy, which I understood. I said, "I know where they are." It really bugged me that on Christmas Eve of all days, when my employee was giving up time with her loved ones to come to work and serve them, those people decided to stiff both me and her. On some other occasion maybe I would have let it go, but this time I thought, "I'm gonna go get that money."

So, I had a dishwasher come with me because I needed a backup. I understood that he worked for me and I had to protect him, so I left him out near the car and told him, "If you hear any gunshots, call the police." I went to the motel room and knocked on the door. I told the guy, "You owe me $128."

He said, "No, we paid it." I said, "No, you didn't." He said, "We paid it with a VISA card." I said, "Nope." Well, they ended up giving me their credit card number. I took it down and called it in when I got back to the restaurant, and it went through. In the hotel room, they had a big gallon jug of Jagermeister sitting on the table and, after all of this, they asked me to do a shot of Jagermeister with them. I went there and got the money out of principle, and then I did a shot with them after I got the money. I protected my business by getting the money that was owed and showing my employees that I wouldn't let things like that go by. I'm there for them.

It was a great Christmas because I stuck up for my baby.

Now, would I do that every day? No, but sometimes, you've just had it. That was my way of protecting my business and protecting what's right. My place could have suffered a $128 loss, but it didn't.

Another time I protected my baby on a much bigger scale. I used to keep a hotel room since I was there every day at the restaurant. I remember one time a customer came in for lunch and drank a double Bloody Mary.

The problem is he had come in drunk.

He only had a little sip of the Bloody Mary. He was an alcoholic, but we didn't know it. My waitress, Donna, had served him not knowing he was drunk. Once you serve that person, however, you become responsible under state law. He drank it. I got back from working out, I pulled in the parking lot, and I saw this guy wandering around. My wife, Sue, saw him and I said, "Let me try to find out what's going on." He was trying to find his car, but he was in no condition to drive. So I asked him, "Well, where's your car?"

He said, "In Vegas." So I said, "I'm going to give you a motel room." I got a key and I didn't register him or anything, but that same night, he tried coming back in the restaurant, but I didn't let him in.

I said, "You can come in and have something to eat, but I'm not going to serve you liquor." I could tell he had a drinking problem. He went out later that night to a package store and bought some vodka. I had to break into the room two days later, where I found him. I felt his pulse and he was dead.

He would've been fine if he hadn't picked up that vodka later and drank himself to death.

I'm sorry he died, but we did everything right after learning he was drunk and unable to drive, but unfortunately my restaurant still got sued for it. I got sued for $750,000, but we were only insured for $500,000.

It was a seven-day trial. We went to court and I told the truth. The family of this guy had me actually stealing money from him, even though he still had $300 on him when the police came to the hotel room.

His daughter claimed I had broken into the room and stolen money from him. She was really working for her attorney, who took the case trying to get her some money out of me. Luckily the jury made the right decision and we won the case. The family proposed a cash settlement, but our insurance company said no. That's protecting my baby in a big way.

It is your responsibility to protect your small business.

If I take two steaks home from my restaurant for dinner, I pay for them. My baby needs that protection.

If you don't feel this way, your baby will struggle. Or worse, you might lose your baby. As a business owner it's easy to gain some success and get too comfortable. You start spending less time at your business and there's no one left to look after your investment the same way you can. There's a reason that I devote so much time and energy to my restaurant, because no matter how well-established Tommy Brann's is, it only takes one wrong move to lose your baby forever.

Side Dish

A Proud Record of Service for 10+ Years

Jennie Lehnertz has been part of Tommy Brann's Steakhouse for 36 years.

She is one of nine faithful employees at the popular neighborhood restaurant on S. Division Avenue in Wyoming who have been on the job for at least 10 years. It's a record of service that makes Brann proud.

"She's a waitress and a supervisor during the lunch hour," Brann said of the trustworthy Lehnertz. "It has been a good run for both of us. She has a good work ethic and she shows up on time. I think she has missed maybe two days in 31 years. That's very unique. It's just the way her parents brought her up."

Other members of the 10+ club at his restaurant:

• Amanda Sanders (27)

• Michelle Roberts (24)

• Jermaine Jennings (22)

• Wyatt Scanson (20)

• Ann Marie Spielmaker (19)

- Laurie Benish (18)

- James Gee (17)

- Jane Prescott (11)

"The loyalty goes both ways," Brann insisted. "I've got dishwashers, waitresses, cooks who've all been here for 10 years. I think people, in general, want to stay in one place. They don't like change.

"If I can provide that security for them in their lives, great."

He is proudest that he has had second generations of families work for him.

"It makes you feel good that maybe you're not a bad boss. It really makes you feel good, someone like Jane Prescott, for example, her daughter, Shanda, works for me now. I think having stability in a company is great," he said. "All of these people know their jobs really well and they've been with me for a long time."

Brann said he hopes that his employees see him as a compassionate leader.

"You're dealing with human beings," he said of handling the ups and downs of leading a restaurant staff. "Every time you have an argument with your boss, you shouldn't get fired for it. If somebody drops a tray of glasses, if I fired somebody for that, how would I feel if I did that? I always try to put myself in that situation.

"You have some power being a boss, but you never want to abuse that power."

"If there is anything a man can do well, I say let him do it. Give him a chance."
—Abraham Lincoln

Chapter 11:
You Can't Do It All Yourself

In the beginning, Tommy Brann's Steakhouse was doing pretty well.

I remember at 19 when I opened my restaurant, my dad did help me a little bit, loaning me $30,000 to get it open, but he also provided me with an important person to help me out. Dick was a bartender at Duck's restaurant and my dad asked him to work for me when I opened my place.

I wanted to control everything. I wanted to be ... not the big shot, but I wanted to demonstrate I was in control of my place. I remember one time Dick told a waitress to make sure to get some water for a table and I got upset at him. Why? He was trying to help me. Tommy Brann's Steakhouse did well from the start, but I was young and I still had some typical 19-year-old immaturity and insecurity issues.

My dad, in his wisdom, had sent Dick, a former manager from one of his stores, to help me. I initially looked at Dick as someone who was trying to take over my job, when he really was just doing his job, which was to help me. It was pretty stupid on my part, but I had some confidence problems and I had to learn.

As a small-business person, it's important to see the bigger picture. You have to be able to accept help and input from other people.

It doesn't mean you're not in control of what's happening in your business. I've learned to take advice and take help from people. In fact, I welcome it and want it. I ask for it. I think it's important. If I had taken help more and delegated better in my early small-business career, I probably would've had an easier life.

I suppose, like all young fathers, I was overly protective of my new "baby."

My first year was pretty hectic. I was single and living in a house on my restaurant property back then. I could never understand people who worked out of their homes. It's hard enough to separate you and your small business, but to actually live on the site? It almost seems impossible. But hey, at least it was a short walk to work.

I had no rent to pay, no gas to buy for the car...and no life outside of work.

Yet, I felt I had a true purpose: to pay my bills and create employment for others. I never thought about becoming a millionaire, but I did want to have security. If I had a slow night at the restaurant, I wanted to know that I had the money in the bank to withstand it. Watching what my dad went through showed me how important it is to have something to fall back on.

It's also important to have the right people surrounding you in your small business.

I want people to be on my side. Now, it doesn't mean you have to say yes to everything and agree with me about everything, but, when push comes to shove, I need to know you are with me. I remember three Christmas Eves in a row – again, we always had an incident on Christmas Eve – this one waitress was checking out her boyfriend who had come in drunk and he was bugging her and getting on our nerves. So I told him to shut up.

We got in a fistfight.

I didn't need any help, but my friend, Tony Kellogg, came and broke us up and threw him outside. I don't forget people who back me up. That was a little extreme, maybe, but, when it comes to people who work for me, I want to have the same feeling: You're there for me and I should not have to explain everything that I'm going to say to you and I should not feel as if I have to tiptoe around you all the time.

I'm still like that after 42 years in the restaurant business.

Drama happens when you own your own business. I inherit a lot of my employees' problems at times. They have an argument at home and come in to wait on my customers in a bad mood. I learned that you have to go with the flow. We are all on stage when we start working and you have good actors and bad actors. It is my job to change the bad actors and that is not easy. Handling what I call "drama" is something that I've learned to do well.

This is going to sound egotistical, but, hypothetically, I think I could be the President of the United States. I really believe I could handle the job. For one thing, the citizens of the United States would never have to question my work ethic. I would also have no problem assembling a cabinet. The way I've learned to take sound advice from trusted sources would serve me well as commander-in-chief. I would get wise experts to act as my secretary of treasury or secretary of energy, people who know more about the issues than I do who can help guide my decisions. I know how to surround myself with people who give me good counsel, and frankly are smarter than me in certain aspects. I don't get defensive and try to do it all on my own like I did when I was a kid. I learned quickly that taking good advice from trusted advisors makes you a more respectable leader, not the other way around.

For instance, I have Janine, a very talented waitress. She is able to take a party of 30 or 40 customers all by herself, so I reward that talent and strength of hers by letting her do that if we get a large group. Is that physical work? Yeah. But she's smarter than me. I couldn't do that. I want more Janines on my team. You should surround yourself with good people and reward the people who do a good job, giving them the incentive to stick around. That's another important business lesson.

It's not just about having people who are talented though. I also surround myself with people I can trust.

Jay Seely, for example, he handles my air conditioning. If Jay says that I should buy this new unit, I know he's selling it to me because that's how he would treat his own restaurant.

You must first surround yourself with the right people then secondly be sure to listen to them.

Side Dish
Our Humble Corporate Headquarters

The first board meetings for Brann's, which were attended by Tom Doyle and my brothers, were pretty humble affairs.

"We used to get together in a motel room. My brothers and I would hold our board meetings here," Tommy Brann said. "I had a 10-unit motel on the property where my restaurant is located on Division Avenue. I remember one meeting when my brothers Johnny and Mike brought Burger King Whoppers and we had a banker in there for that meeting. We had a toilet seat in there, too, which was for remodeling or something. It was one of the most unprofessional settings, but it worked for us at the time.

"We met in those rooms for quite a while and we made a couple of those rooms into professional offices," he said of the motel, which was later demolished to make room for more parking spaces.

The Brann's Corporation ended up getting a little fancier for its board meetings.

"We later moved to our catering place, which also is located further down South Division Avenue, and we went downstairs, but we still didn't have the best area," Tommy Brann said of their modest accommodations. "Our corporate headquarters is now located at 25 Commerce Ave. downtown in Grand Rapids. We moved there about five years ago and that's a 100-percent professional place for us."

Still, there's no mahogany conference table for the first family of Sizzling Steaks.

The Brann's corporate headquarters occupies the basement of a building that is simple but tasteful, much like the family-owned chain of restaurants that has become part of the West Michigan landscape.

"Yeah, it was very humble beginnings for us at our board meetings – about as humble as you can get."

"It is rare to find a business partner who is selfless. If you are lucky, it happens once in a lifetime."
—Michael Eisner

Chapter 12:

How to Catch a Frog Leg Thief

I had a lot of good people working for me when I started my small business.

Some of my employees were my age, but everyone took their orders from a 19-year-old kid, which must have been difficult at times, especially since I had a lot to learn. Frank VanNorman, my first cook at Tommy Brann's Steakhouse, is the biggest reason I've gone so far.

There are a lot of lessons I learned from him.

Frank had been working at The Southern when my dad and I bought it. He was a good man. My dad's business sense really kicked in and he told me to keep Frank on the payroll while we were in the process of remodeling. My dad was a good judge of character and he could see that Frank would be great for me.

Frank helped me so much while we were preparing to open.

He cared about my new business and worked hard for me. Frank had two jobs. He worked at a factory called Kelvinator during the day and then came to work for me at night at the restaurant. He was there every night. He always worked hard and he was honest. I could not have asked for a better babysitter for my new baby.

He cooked for me and took care of my kitchen, which is the heartbeat of any restaurant. He became my go-to person with great problem solving skills, so I was very fortunate to have a man like him in my corner. He made the business seem less lonely. He reinforced the critical lesson that in every company, what it boils down to is good people. It sometimes is the hardest thing to get right, but when you make a good choice, it all becomes easier with good people taking care of your business the same way you would take care of it.

I wouldn't be here right now without the support of Frank VanNorman.

Among his many other talents, he had a real knack for catching thieves.

Imagine giving a person a job. You pay them and then they end up stealing from you. They're stealing from your business, your baby. It feels like a betrayal. Frank was outstanding at catching them. Over the years, Frank must have caught more than a dozen employees who were stealing from me, and he did it to protect my business.

I wasn't naïve about the fact that people wanted to take from me, but Frank had that keen radar and solid work ethic that made him especially good at catching the thieves. He was on salary for me, but even then he said, "Let's open for business Sundays because I think we'll do pretty good." Because of him, we actually opened Sundays, although most restaurants were closed on Sundays back then. We went back and forth with the experiment of being open on Sundays, but ultimately we found that it was a really good idea. That's how much dedication Frank had to the business. He was always thinking of ways that we could do better and gain more success. He had loyalty and honesty and he had my utmost trust in him.

One of Frank's biggest claims to fame was catching the frog leg thief.

Believe it or not, I actually had an employee stealing frog legs from me. It was this cook and he ran his scam by parking his car just beyond the kitchen where boxes of food came in and out. It was a pretty decent trick, but not good enough to get past Frank. Even before we saw the direct evidence, Frank knew. He wouldn't let people buffalo him. He'd say, "Nah, you got 'em. You took 'em." Sure enough, the frog legs were stashed in the back seat of this guy's car.

He sensed what was happening and he took control of the situation.

He probably caught twice as many people stealing from me as I did in my own place, and I was no slouch at catching thieves myself.

He was a good babysitter. He treated my restaurant like it was his own baby. Boy, did that make things a lot easier for me. He already had a lot of business lessons in him, lessons that he shared with me.

Frank echoed my dad's advice about learning to go with the flow, which among all the lessons that I've learned over the years has become the focal point of my 13 business principles.

Eventually Frank left my place to take a job at Steelcase, which I understood because it provided him with a pension and it was a better job for him in that regard. Even though he's retired from Steelcase he works at the airport now. He likes people so much, he decided to get a job after retirement that allowed him to interact with folks all the time. He doesn't do it for the money. He likes being active and social. That's my idea of good character and a strong work ethic.

The staff at Tommy Brann's Steakhouse liked Frank. He is a great human being. It wasn't like he was looking for it all the time, but he had that special sixth sense when it came to catching thieves. I had it back then too, but sometimes in business you lose that edge.

Timing also has a lot to do with it. I remember one time walking back to my liquor room where I found two high school kids who I had working for me. One was at the door. I kept walking past because I'm a fast-paced guy, but of course they weren't supposed to be in that room in the first place and when I circled back I saw the other kid taking a case of liquor out the door. I caught them.

I didn't do anything at first because the kids were football players and I didn't want to screw up their lives. I did catch them and make them put the liquor back, and I kept a close eye on them after that. In your business, it's important to keep moving in different areas of your operation so you see what's happening as much as possible at all times. The more ever-present you are, the more likely you are to keep your employees honest, if for no other reason than they know you're always there and they could easily get caught.

I was the youngest restaurateur in the state of Michigan at age 19 when I first opened, and Frank VanNorman helped me a lot. He also cared about me and I cared about him. I was good for him and he was good for me.

The word "business" sometimes is a cold word. I'd actually like to change "business" in the Webster's Dictionary. If Mr. Webster were still alive, I'd say, "Can we change the word 'business?'" He described it correctly, but the word "business" has come to mean something different to a lot of people. It has gotten the reputation of being just a profitable enterprise, especially in big business, where it's about greed and not caring about poor people.

It's so much the opposite of that in small business. I'd change the word "business" to "job creating" or "team building." It's about human beings. In the instance of Frank VanNorman, it was a mutually beneficial relationship. He was so good for me that I created a Grand Rapids Community College scholarship fund for African-American culinary students in his honor, and because he was my friend.

Anyone who insists "business" is bad or "business" is a code word for nothing but greed probably doesn't understand. To me, "business" is all about good people being part of it.

In my restaurant, Frank VanNorman was simply the best of people.

Side Dish
The Irrepressible Dave Rozema

A frequent patron of Tommy Brann's Steakhouse during his Major League Baseball playing career was Dave Rozema, a former Grand Rapids Central High School standout who earned a 1984 World Series championship ring. He became a wallflower at Brann's whenever he stopped off for some liquid refreshment.

"I think he's the most personable celebrity we've had in here," Brann said. "I always rooted for Dave when he pitched because he was a local guy. He came in and he was drinking White Russians and he would come into my office and he was very personable. He sort of became part of the place for a couple of hours.

"That's how magnetizing he was. He came in while he was still pitching for the Tigers."

Rozy, as he is affectionately called, regaled the staff and customers with baseball stories and a larger-than-life personality.

"Of all the celebrities, he was the most easy to know," Brann said. "I thought it was really classy the way he handled himself in a fun way, not stuck up or anything like that. He'd joke around, use the phone, he just took over."

"The greatest ability in business is to get along with others and to influence their actions."
—*John Hancock*

Chapter 13:
Romance in the Workplace

I met my future wife, Sue, at Tommy Brann's Steakhouse. She was looking for a job.

My father-in-law still lives across the street from the restaurant. He has been there for approximately 65 years. He's 93 years old. His daughter, Sue, came in looking for work. I was about 20 years old at the time and running for Wyoming City Council. I recall asking her if she was a registered voter before I even hired her. I was half-joking, of course, but she was a registered voter in Wyoming.

I did hire her, and I know there are a lot of strict laws, and I'm not saying they're wrong, but some people do meet their future spouses in the workplace. I've had waitresses' daughters meet their boyfriends at my restaurant. I've had several employees through the years meet, get married and have families. Some-times, in small businesses, it just happens and I won't apologize for that. Do we have a policy against it? Yes, a semi-policy, but people fall in love and I can't help but make exceptions for that. In fact, it makes me happy that so many of my employees have found love through my restaurant. I'm especially happy that I met my soul mate in that same way.

Sue was a great waitress and a wonderful person. She proved herself as a good employee so no one ever questioned whether I was giving her special treatment because of our romantic involvement. Her strong work ethic is one of the reasons why I fell in love with her. I still did not change my own work ethic once we got involved, but I loved being with her whenever possi-ble. Anyway, I don't think she would have wanted me to change. The 20-year-old workaholic restaurant owner was the man she fell in love with in the first place. I was focused on Tommy Brann's Steakhouse. I had to be — my baby was only 3 years old when Sue and I tied the knot. Owning a restaurant is one of the toughest jobs there is. Rich DeVos, co-founder of Am-way Corporation, once said of restaurants: "Everyone should own one — to get it done with." So many people want to be in the restaurant business because their mom makes a good lasagna or grandmother made great meatballs. They enjoy cooking at home with a glass of wine and maybe they can even make a great dinner for 8, so they think, "Hey, I should do this for a living," but Rich knew that it isn't nearly that simple. Try it once and get it out of your system. You will find that it's not all the ease and glory that it might seem like from the outside.

My nephew read an article in National Geographic which stated that being a restaurant owner is one of the toughest jobs in the world. If you own a small business, you have to be a special person. You have to be able to handle a different crisis every day. You might have backed up toilets on Mother's Day, which I've had. You might lose electricity on Valentine's Day, which has happened. You might have dishwashers walk out during the dinner rush, which has happened. Your cook might come into work drunk. Your bartenders might be putting money in their own pockets instead of in the cash register. Your cleanup crews might not show up. Your customers might act up on occasion and get into bar fights...all of which can occur while you are working seven days a week.

You are not just a restaurant owner and manager. You are a part-time security guard, psychologist, nurse, doctor, plumber, carpenter, caretaker of your business and, more than anything else, its primary babysitter.

The challenges are so overwhelming at times that it makes you wonder why anyone would want to do it.

As I write this, I actually feel like I can't really answer that.

It's a slow Sunday night in late October and last night was not that great, either. I am sitting alone worrying about my baby. And, like having a child, you never stop worrying about your business, although a lot of people find that hard to understand. In any profession, you will have your doubts and questions, but those concerns are magnified when you are the owner. I think that's why I appreciate my wife so much.

Sue and I have been married for more than 38 years.

I was 22 when we got married. You still have to dedicate your time and effort to your business or else you can't support your wife and family, but I'm no longer there at 2 a.m. a lot of the time like I used to be.

Still, no matter what, you're always thinking about your business somewhere in the back of your mind, even when you're not there.

I do have one regret about the past with my wife. We got married on a Sunday just so that I wouldn't have to miss a Saturday night of work. Upon reflection, that was just plain wrong on my part. That's just not right. She is on my side, being the wife of a small-business owner. When things happen in the business, she understands it and gets it. Having her support is of great comfort to me, and my life would be so much harder without her dedication. She never made me choose between her and my baby.

It can be lonely when you're running your own restaurant. Sometimes, you feel like your customers and your employees are against you. You sometimes feel like you're the only one babysitting this place.

The place is out there on its own if you're not there. When I'm gone I feel like I've abandoned it a little bit. Every business has that one person who really cares about it. I remember reading Apple Inc. co-founder, chairman and CEO Steve Jobs' book, which wasn't even really about money. He cared about his company and really wanted it to be the best that it could be. He's the one who came back and cared about that company after it went through some tough times.

Even when they booted him out, he kept one share of stock so he was still a part of his company. Upon returning, he proved it by bringing it back to life. I never met Steve Jobs, but I'm sure there were times when he felt pretty lonely. You do feel like you're the only one who really gets it.

I'm blessed that my wife Sue, whom I love dearly, has been there to help me through it all, good times and difficult times. Being in the bar business, I see all types of people and they're not all good.

My wife is a good human being.

I also love my dog, Howie, and all my past dogs. The goodness in them helps bring me back from those lonely feelings at times. I've seen servers stealing from each other. I've seen customers doing rotten things to other customers. I've seen a lot of negative things in this business. Part of it is just humans being human. I've also seen a lot of great things. I try to focus on the good and not just the negative. I don't want my experience as a small business owner to be like high school, where the person who does a bad thing stands out, while the teacher doesn't even know the names of the other 20 students in the class sometimes. I appreciate the employees and customers who bring positivity to my place.

I think it's important to share all of those feelings with your spouse, the good and the bad.

At first, I didn't do that. I kept the struggles of being a small-business owner and young restaurateur bottled up inside. I thought it was the macho thing to do: Keep it within yourself, you're the head of the business, why should she have to know what you went through, a cook walking out or any of the other minor disasters that happen on a regular basis.

I didn't share those things with her at first, but she voiced her opinion about it. This happened about 30 years ago. I listened to her and took that so-called machismo and began instead to share things with her, and it really has been great for me to include her in those things. Up until then I hadn't given her enough credit for how much she could handle, and I underestimated how good it would feel to me to have someone else shoulder a little bit of the burden, just by being there to listen.

The only mistake she made at first was playing devil's advocate sometimes. I don't like that. She used to do it a lot, but I asked her not to do it anymore. Instead of presenting both sides, I wanted to start out with her being on my side. I need more people on my side. To her credit she listened to me and she doesn't do that anymore.

I'm grateful and blessed, for all of the times I listened to my wife and it has been the right decision. Having her in my life is one of the best gifts that my business ever gave me.

Side Dish
The Gateway Project

The next time you're passing through the intersection of 28th Street and Division Avenue, steal a momentary glance at the impressive plaza with five flags proudly displayed that connects Grand Rapids and Wyoming.

It's called the Gateway Project and a proud part of Tommy Brann's legacy.

He was instrumental in helping transform a non-descript piece of property overlooking a congested intersection that people might never notice into something everyone from both communities can be proud of.

"I wanted to put a business sign up there because I was president of the Division Avenue Association. It was supposed to be just a business sign on MDOT property on the northeast corner across from the Belt-line Bar," he said. "I wanted to put up a sign saying, 'Welcome to Division Avenue Businesses' and welcoming people into our district. So, I got ahold of a few people. It just shows you, as a small-business lesson, if you surround yourself with good people, there's no telling what you might be able to accomplish.

"I lucked out in this way when I surrounded myself with Bob Dekker, who was the Burton Heights Business Association leader, and Neighborhood Ventures, which is a non-profit organization that takes on projects like this and helps you get funds for it," he explained. "I had this idea and it just started to blossom."

It went from being a simple sign to becoming a grand statement.

"We turned it into the Gateway Project, which meant that we added five flags to represent the state of Michigan, both cities, Grand Rapids and Wyoming, Kent County, and the United States flag is there," he said. "It also has a wall that contains the logos of the cities of Grand Rapids and Wyoming, and we actually took it one step further and had some railroad trestles painted that say Welcome to Wyoming and Welcome to Grand Rapids. It just blossomed and it's a great project there we're all proud of."

It took two years to secure $250,000 in funding to complete the project.

"We got grants and we went to different organizations," Brann said. "It's one of the times Grand Rapids and Wyoming worked together on a project."

"The business schools reward difficult complex behavior more than simple behavior, but simple behavior is more effective."
—Warren Buffett

Chapter 14:
Keeping It Simple

As a 19-year-old kid, I did all of my own ordering for the restaurant.

I was a hands-on small-business owner all the way. I was like a new mother who would never leave her newborn child alone. I took on that same affection and dedication for my newborn business. While my friends were living normal lives, I worked seven days a week at Tommy Brann's Steakhouse.

I liked to keep my food orders low and would sometimes skip an order so that I could rotate my product and keep my bill low. It was common sense. No real business procedure or analysis had to be involved. I did what worked for me.

The lesson is that sometimes the right decision for your business is not that hard to make, but I find that the restaurant business has become more complex. Of course, complexity can kill a business, so I find that I am fighting the bigger picture more and more these days to try to make the business simpler to run. I learned a long time ago from my father that the right decision is not hard to make. I don't do my own ordering. I could do it, yes, but it's more complex now.

It's probably 75 percent more complex as far as ordering and liquor. In the old days, our biggest-selling beer at my dad's place was Pabst Blue Ribbon. You'd sell five or six different brands of beer: Goebel's, Pabst, and Budweiser mainly, but no light beers. Meister Brau Light was the first light beer we served in the restaurant.

Now, you've got so many beers and so many liquors. That's nobody's fault, but it's something that adds to the complexity of this business. It has made it harder. You still have to limit what brands you sell.

One habit of mine that's served me well is writing down my ideas as they come to me. I might write things down at 1 a.m. It doesn't mean it's going to get done at 2 a.m., but I feel like I'm on the way to maybe getting that goal accomplished.

I read an article on running a business and four important things about it. One of the four factors they listed was "book smarts," which they stated was not very important for business ownership, and I tend to agree. One of the other things was about passion, and I think that's an overused word, but my point is I was a 19-year-old kid when I opened my restaurant. I couldn't have taken that leap at such a young age if I wasn't passionate about the restaurant industry and small business ownership. What I lacked in book smarts I made up for in drive and common sense, and I think those attributes served me better than anything I could have learned in college. During the four years that I would have spent in school, reading textbooks on what it means to be a business owner, I was right in the thick of it, learning new things every day. Maybe I made some mistakes that I wouldn't have made if I'd learned about economics or corporate structures in school, but the lessons I learned from my missteps were so concrete, so real, that I never made the same mistake again.

For instance, I don't think I needed to go to college to learn how to manage my food order. I remember looking at my cooler on a Sunday night and saying, "I don't need a produce order. I can get by." It's sort of back to my dad's common sense, that the simple system of rotating food keeps me from having to throw away perfectly good product and having to place a whole new order before I really need it. It saves on waste and it saves on cost. Since that time, I've seen this technique recommended in books about restaurant management, but it's something that I learned from my dad, and it's also my first instinct. The lesson learned is that sometimes business decisions are simple acts guided by common sense as opposed to overthinking things.

None of this is to say that a college education isn't important, but in some situations and in certain industries, practical experience and common sense are more important. Sometimes, you need to have confidence in yourself. If you didn't go to college, you still need to believe in your ability to solve a problem and stand by the decisions you make. Thanks to the training I got from working with my dad, and a dash of natural ability, I had that confidence when I got into this business at age 19. When I read textbooks on my own time I usually found that the business practices that they were teaching were things that I was already doing. People learn the ropes in different ways, but for me "book smarts" wasn't part of the equation. I didn't have textbooks. I had practical experience and common sense, and, in the end, whether you go to college or not, there's no substitute for that.

Side Dish
The Donut Guy

One of the proudest accomplishments later in life for Tommy Brann has been enlisting in the Michigan Volunteer Defense Force, which helps support the state police in times of state emergencies.

"I'm a specialist in the Michigan Volunteer Defense Force. I always felt like I didn't serve my country. It's a regret. I could've done it, but I chose to be stuck here at the restaurant, so no excuses," he said.

At one of his first meetings, he volunteered for an important assignment.

"As part of my duties as a specialist, when I first volunteered, they asked, 'Well, who wants to bring donuts and coffee to our meetings?' Nobody was raising their hand, so, I figured, I'm new here, I figured I should do it since I'm in the restaurant business," he recalled. "So, I raised my hand, and ever since then I've been 'The Donut Guy.'

"Every meeting, it's my responsibility to bring the donuts. I take care of the funds for it, and we even try to make a little profit off it. I bring them from Marge's Donut Den in Wyoming sometimes. Other times, since

I'm a frugal guy, I'll go get day-old donuts so we can make a little more profit off them."

You are required to wear a uniform after enlisting in the state defense force.

Yet, for Brann, it was a difficult for him to feel comfortable putting on a military uniform because he felt he hadn't earned that privilege – not like friends from high school who ended up going off to war earlier in life.

"You get a uniform as part of the Michigan Volunteer Defense Force. I told them, 'I don't think I've earned it,' but they said, 'Tom, you have to get a uniform.' I didn't feel comfortable, but my wife, Sue, told me I needed to own that," he said. "I just never compared myself to my friends who served in Vietnam. But, I did, I got a uniform."

The first time he put on a uniform to attend a meeting, he had butterflies in his stomach.

"I remember the first time I brought the donuts in uniform to our meeting," he said. "I remember walking up there and thinking, 'What if somebody salutes?' I was still learning the customs and traditions of the armed forces. I kept thinking, 'What if there's a colonel out here? What do I do when I see him? Do I salute or not?'

"Sure enough, I pull up and the guards out front are talking and I'm a little nervous about the whole thing. But I had my hands full of boxes of donuts. I learned later that's a good thing. So, they saluted me. They didn't know I was just a private at that time, so I acknowledged them with a head shake and kept on going because I had my hands full. I learned after the fact if your hands are full, you don't have to salute.

"It was a lucky break, but it was nerve-wracking," he added. "I'm still learning a lot of the armed forces protocols. My fellow military friends told me when in doubt, be sure to salute. I've been in the Michigan Volunteer Defense Force for about five or six years, and I'm still bringing the donuts to our meetings. Two years ago, they got me a gigantic donut at our Christmas party. I had to put it in the freezer."

"I definitely did look up to John. We all looked up to John. He was older and he was very much the leader; he was the quickest wit and the smartest."
—*Paul McCartney*

Chapter 15:
Our Fab Four

A lot of people wonder about the relationships between us Brann brothers.

Well, it's not the Brady Bunch, not at all. I'd com-
pare the relationships between myself, Johnny Brann,
who owns and operates Brann's-Leonard Street, Mike
Brann, who operates Brann's-Cascade, and Tom
Doyle, who operates Brann's-Grandville, to that of the
Beatles...my all-time favorite band.

If for some reason the Beatles had come to me for
business advice when they were thinking of splitting
up I would have said, "Let's keep Apple Records together and let's still be friends, but let's all go our separate ways from time to time." Why not go your separate ways and then maybe they'd come back some day
and work together again? I know, who am I to be giv-

ing advice to the Beatles. They managed to be pretty successful without my sage counsel, but I am very proud of the way that my partners and I have managed to work together for the good of our company and everyone involved.

One of the positive things about Brann's corporate structure is we don't work together every day in the same office. We are going our separate ways, but we're still working together. I really think that that separation and independence is crucial to our success as partners. It's a nice recipe because everybody's got their own space and time. Again, if we were a musical group, we would record together and then take lots of time off in between, not be on tour every day in the same hotel room, getting on each other's nerves and getting upset about who's got the dirty socks that smell.

I will say, though, for as much as we've worked out a good system, it hasn't been like a Christmas Story as far as our relationships with each other either.

One time, I showed my wife, Sue, a Christmas calendar we had put together and it had a little restaurant on it and you could see the little 1952 trucks there with the little snow tracks. It really was a cool calendar. I told my wife, Sue, you could even see the waitresses working in the restaurant around the Christmas season. But, knowing the ins and outs of the industry like I did, the sweet image didn't look the same to me. Looking at it with Sue, I said to her, "First of all, you see a customer walking out on a check. Second of all, there's a plumbing problem and there's a toilet overflowing. The cook is mad. They're one waitress short because she didn't show up and she didn't call anyone to replace her." Sue said, "Wow!" I was going through the entire business being Mr. Negative.

I suppose that's the type of business we're in, or maybe it's any industry where you have to mix personal relationships with business. It's not always wonderful because we're in this business together.

Although we'll always be linked through our corporate relationship, we do go our separate ways indirectly.

I love Johnny and Mike, my brothers, and Tom Doyle, who's been with us a long time. If something happened to them, I would definitely be there for each of them. I don't always agree with them on ideology. It's sort of like politics. You don't agree with everyone on everything. Sometimes you argue over your differences and try to bring the other person around to your way of seeing things, but other times you accept that you'll never see eye-to-eye and you let it go. I do get a little more say in the final decisions for our company because I'm the president and I'm the one who got us together. I feel like I've earned that right, but I also try to be fair and diplomatic in my dealings with the other guys. I know that I'm not always right about everything, and I also care about all of them on a personal level.

Things between us didn't always run as smoothly as they do now. It took time. We used to have separate menus, separate insurance companies, a lot of things separate. At a certain point I got my father and brothers together and I remember telling them, "We have got to work together. We have to consolidate if we want Brann's to survive." It was hard to let go of some of that independence, but it was what was best for the company, which means it's what was best for us.

Making the decision to work together more required me to go back to a little bit of my dad's common sense. I wanted us to be bigger, better, more professional, and in order to do that we had to consolidate some things. For a long time we even had separate insurance companies! Coming together on even that one thing saved us a lot of money and hassle.

I remember talking to Gordon Food Service, which had a better rate if you ordered 55 items or more back then. I sometimes ordered 40 items, but I said, "We have two other places and they have 20 other items, so can we combine this?" I had one partner who insisted it would never happen, but it did happen. To their credit, Gordon Food Service told me, "Yeah, we'll do it." It was easy because they listened to me and they understood where I was coming from. It's a tough business we're in, and most people on the outside don't know just how difficult it can be to make things run smoothly and turn a profit, but my brothers and Tom Doyle understand completely. Despite the difficulty of working with other people and different viewpoints, it's nice to know that we're in it together.

For the most part, there's not much disagreement between the four of us. If something is reasonable and makes our business more profitable, there's not much of a discussion. In the end, as separate as we may be, there's little debating common sense.

We do, however, have different arrangements throughout the Brann's restaurant chain.

I own my place, Tommy Brann's, at 4157 S. Division Ave. in Wyoming 100 percent. Johnny owns his place, Mike and Johnny Brann's, at 401 Leonard St. NW in Grand Rapids 100 percent The rest we all own together as partners, including my brother Mike who runs his place at 5510 28th St. SE in Grand Rapids near Cascade, and Tom Doyle who runs his place at 3475 Fairlanes Ave. SW in Grandville. Mike left the business to work for Domestic Linen as a driver. He came back to Burton Heights to help my dad run his restaurant. I always admired Mike for the courage it took to leave the business. He left because the demanding hours kept him from his young family.

It is a different arrangement. As a result, I don't think our board meetings have always worked for us. They have not been efficient, they last too long, and that's my fault since I'm the leader.

It's not something I'd pattern it after, our board meetings, but it boils down to most decisions are common sense. You can say it's just business, but it's not. It's personal.

I'll explain our roles in terms of the four members of the Beatles.

Johnny is our Paul McCartney. I like that description of him because he's really into the business and marketing. The personal side of me is so happy that he's happy in this business, yet the business side of me disagrees with him sometimes. Our relationship, like any partnership, is strained sometimes, but of course, all in all, there is no doubting that I love my brothers.

Mike is sort of the George Harrison of Brann's. You recall that George was often referred to as the nice Beatle. He's just a good human being. Although the people in my life are very important to me, Mike is a bit more family-oriented, whereas I put business first and know that my family understands. That's caused some tension in our relationship at times, but I respect Mike's commitment to his personal life. He's a great guy and we've actually become closer over the past two years.

Tom Doyle is our Ringo Starr. He's a late comer to the group. You recall that Ringo replaced Pete Best, the original drummer of the Beatles. The band got rid of Pete Best because he was too good looking and he was getting all the girls. Tom used to work for me as a busboy at Tommy Brann's Steakhouse. He represents another important business lesson learned about working your way up in an organization.

I was 19 and he was 17 when I opened my restaurant. Tom came with the place, called The Southern, that I bought. He went to Michigan State University. It's yet another instance in which I was able to surround myself with smart people. When I talk about taking the advice of wise consultants, Tom is one of the guys I think of first. He had a college education and he came back and ran our Alpine Brann's location and did some great things there. He took over a location, probably in 1978, where we were $30,000 in the hole. That was a lot of money at that time. He helped bring it back and took a personal interest in that store,   although it no longer exists. He's a savvy businessman and a very good friend. He now runs the Brann's-Grandville location.

I would say I'm the John Lennon of the group because I'm the leader. I'm the one who got the band together. Talent-wise, we all have Paul McCartney talent. I think it's spread evenly across the four of us. I'd give Paul McCartney to Johnny because it's well-deserved. He has been a good leader when it comes to small things like a twice-baked potato or mushrooms and onions as an add-on for steaks, and those details are part of what makes the difference between a good restaurant and a great restaurant.

It might seem like a small thing to a customer, but, even before he got into marketing, Johnny was the member of the group who brought up mushrooms and onions, putting them on our menu and selling them as an extra item. That's creative and that's innovative. Of course we're just a few small business owners in Michigan, not international superstars, but I've always liked thinking of our business dynamic in terms of the Beatles, and the roles seem to fit.

In the past, there have been issues that divided the family.

I enjoy my leadership role and I take the responsibility seriously. As talented as my business partners are, it still takes a John Lennon to bring them back and rein them in if somebody is playing accordion in the background at one of our concerts. It's like, "What's that about?" We don't always agree on everything. It takes organization to keep us all on the same stage, and I'll take credit for that.

You're dealing with human beings and egos, and even John Lennon decided to give up being the leader of the Beatles eventually. Paul McCartney became too overbearing for him. Now, McCartney did some great things for the Beatles, but it was difficult for them to maintain that balance of friendship, creativity, and business. There's only so much you can control, especially when it comes to family being involved in the same business. The only way you can keep it all together is if your business partners have consideration for you. In the past, we've had it where we've all been a bunch of cowboys riding off in different directions. Actually, recently, the past two years, have been difficult. It's not healthy for the company when that happens. You have to have a posse and you have to be organized to do it right.

In addition to all of that, my two nephews, Johnny Jr. and Mike Jr., are part of the family business as well.

Johnny Jr., he absorbs things and he learns a lot. He also can be a teacher, although he's much younger. I've become close to Johnny Jr. I did tell him because of his fast-casual concept restaurant, the recently opened Kitchen 67 Brann's Cafe, located at 1977 East Beltline NE in Grand Rapids, that "he's running away from our business." I meant it as a compliment. He is trying to take the Brann's concept to another level.

It's probably another business lesson learned: You can say things that are pretty bold, but "running away from our business" shouldn't be taken as a negative thing because our business is really hard to run. We have more than 70 items on our menu. We have a lot of employees at our restaurants. He's moving away from that concept by having fewer items on the menu and less employees. It's really a smart thing to do.

I think that's why "fast-casual" is catching on, because it's much like the proliferation of self-serve gas stations. If you own a gas station and you've got a guy calling in sick every day, you're pumping gas and you think, "I'm gonna let the customer pump the gas." That's what fast-causal is; he's letting the customer pump the gas. It's a great thing for him and it's even greater for customers because it gets them out faster.

In a different way, Kitchen 67 could be the next evolution of the Brann's restaurant. The jury's still out on that. We've had some long conversations about it. The concepts are different. It's a smart run, though. You're always looking for ways to reinvent yourself and make an impression on customers or potential new customers.

Let's go back to the Beatles again.

If they wanted to keep singing, "I Want to Hold Your Hand," something like "Sgt. Pepper's Lonely Hearts Club Band" never would've happened. You have to change. We've gone from red carpet to relish trays to hot-food bars to salad bars to specials, which we never had, to steak and lobster, which we never specialized in. You have to always evolve. If you don't, as a business, you are going to sink.

It has been extremely difficult at times to keep family and business separate. In the past, we have been separated as a family during the holidays over disagreements about the business. It does get personal.

I think we ought to have our menu items limited a little bit more and we need to have more control in that area. Another partner who doesn't work in the restaurant every day says, "Whatever it takes, it doesn't matter." Well, it does matter. I'm in the restaurant every day. I'm the John Lennon of the group. Is this the music I wanna play? No, I don't want to play some of that music. So, how can that not be personal?

The partnership is the area most affected by the rule that you can't separate business and emotion completely. It's always personal, especially when you have to make business decisions with family members and friends.

However, when it comes to the board room, it's business first, not family. I don't think, as brothers or as partners in our company, we're ever totally apart. We run our company like a democracy. Although it's personal, when it comes to each of us running our businesses, we're never apart. If something happened to my brother Mike or my brother Johnny, the things we argue over like the mashed potatoes that Johnny wants to put on and I don't want to put on the menu, that sort of stuff would immediately lose importance.

Just like any other democracy, it's not always perfect and it doesn't work 100 percent of the time. It's still the best form of government there is, though, right? I mean, in one way it seems like the only way to do it, but there are companies that have a little bit of a dictatorship that are successful, like Steve Jobs when he did Apple the second time around. He appointed his own board, he took over and look what happened. Democracies are tougher. If we do leave the conference room at the Brann's corporate office and I've lost a key vote, it might not be a key vote to the customer, but it affects my life very directly. If I put another item on the menu that was voted in by other partners who are not on the front lines but in the board room in a cushy seat, I still I have to stock and put away and cook that menu item myself. If someone votes for a change that doesn't affect them as much as it does me, then it grinds me.

It grinds me when I know I'm right. I'm sure they feel the same way about me but that doesn't stop us from working together, because regardless of some battles that I lose, our partnership makes Brann's a better company, and I'll do anything for my baby.

Side Dish
The Other Brann Brother

The three Brann brothers in the restaurant business – Tommy, Johnny Jr. and Mike — are well known throughout the West Michigan area, but a fourth brother, Joe, has also been a part of the family legacy.

Joe Brann started out as a cook at his father's restaurant in Burton Heights.

He was right there alongside older brothers Tommy, Johnny and Mike while helping establish John Brann's Steakhouse as one of the popular local eateries when it first opened in 1961 and touted its Sizzling Steaks.

"Joe is my youngest brother. He started out in the restaurant business," Tommy Brann said.

"He was great for my dad as far as a cook. He worked at John Brann's Steakhouse in Burton Heights. So did my brothers Johnny and Mike. The only member of the family who didn't work there was my sister Liz, who's the youngest of the children," he added. "Joe was a good cook; he just didn't like the business as much as the rest of us."

Instead, Joe Brann pursued a career in local real estate.

"He went to our old Alpine Avenue location and helped run it for a while," Tommy Brann recalled, "but he was more into real estate. He liked buying and selling things. That was his forte. I give him credit for leaving the restaurant business and doing something else. It got him out of his comfort zone."

Not long ago, Joe returned to the family restaurant business, joining the staff of the Brann's location in Holland.

"He serves as a host at the Holland restaurant and he does a great job," Tommy Brann said. "He treats people really nice and people really like him."

"I am certainly not one of those who needs to be prodded. In fact, if anything, I am the prod."
—Winston Churchill

Chapter 16:
Supporting Free Enterprise

I organized a rally Dec. 12, 2011, in downtown Grand Rapids for free enterprise.

Luckily, although it was a winter day, the sun was out. We had 125 people there. I'm a free-enterprise advocate. I get involved politically and I support people involved in free enterprise like our recent vice presidential nominee, Congressman Paul Ryan of Wisconsin, and local business leaders such as Peter Secchia, former U.S. Ambassador to Italy and former chairman of Universal Forest Products, and Rich DeVos, Amway Corp. co-founder.

I'm so tired of the saying about class warfare and rich people not caring about other people. I want to get a class on free enterprise into the school systems so that other Tommy Branns can emerge. There's no reason a C-average student can't own his own business, there's no reason a C-average student can't own his own hardware store. Of course, he or she can. It might not happen, though, if no one shows them the ropes or informs them that it's a realistic option.

I want them to hire people. I want them to understand when they hire someone what it costs to hire that person. I want the little details to be put into our students' minds so they understand what our country was built on, which is free enterprise. It's the only economic system we should be part of in the United States.

One hundred million people from China have been lifted out of poverty there because of free enterprise. That's from an article I read in Time Magazine about three years ago. So, that's one of my future goals. My business has made me into who I am today, and I would never want to apologize for that.

Free enterprise has taken it on the chin in recent years in this country.

When I decided to set up the rally in downtown Grand Rapids, I wasn't against anybody, I was just for something. You had the so-called 1 percent of small-business owners being bad-mouthed in the media. Nobody else was having a rally for free enterprise. I dare say we were the only one in the country that had a rally for free enterprise. I had the Rolling Stones' song "You Can't Always Get What You Want," which was the first thing played. I was a speaker, as was Denny Gilliem, Tom Doyle, Fulton Sheen and Tim Doctor. It lasted almost an hour. I was somewhat worried about it, because there were only five people at about 10 minutes to noon who showed up at Calder Plaza. I said, "Oh, boy." But people came through. It was called Ten to Defend and I issued 10 reasons for defending free enterprise.

I also did a radio show on WJRW-AM 1340 called "Mind Your Own Business" in 2011. It started out with local radio legend Kevin Matthews and we did it on a Saturday morning, but the listening audience is small at that time of day. I went back to them and said, "Can I do something different?" I interviewed friends in the small-business community and that was fun. It was a live call-in show, which was fun. We talked about politics and Pete Hoekstra called in when he was running for governor.

We had politicians on and I actually was going up against Rush Limbaugh, and that was fun because Grand Rapids all of a sudden had Rush Limbaugh billboards put up after my show went on the air. It wasn't because of me those billboards went up, but it was kind of humorous that it happened at the same time.

It was an hour-long show and we had a good time. It was all about free enterprise. Creating a job is a compassionate thing. You're paying for somebody's social security, which is their retirement, and you're paying for their Medicare, so every hour they work you're contributing to their health care and their pension plan. How can that be a bad thing to do? I don't care if it's a minimum-wage job or what, that's never a bad thing to do.

Embrace free enterprise. It's the only way the country is going to survive. You need free enterprise for the government to survive. Embrace it and unleash it. When Pete Hoekstra was running for governor, he loved that quote of mine. Unleash businesses. I love my dog. You go to the park and unleash your dog and see how much fun he has running free. They go up to little kids and the kids come up and pet them. A lot of good things happen if you're unleashed. It's the same thing with small businesses.

It doesn't mean there shouldn't be regulations. You need regulations, like you do for a dog park, but if dogs, or small businesses, are tied up the whole time, you're not going to have a bunch of happy dogs or a groups of successful small-business owners. You have some unhappy owners nowadays because they're leashed too tight.

In May of 2013 Senator Levin brought Apple in front of a Senate committee to ask them why they ship 100 billion dollars overseas to avoid taxes in this country. It's an example of a long time Senator out of touch with free enterprise and the tax system he helped create. It's an over-regulated system containing over 70,000 pages of tax code. Senator Rand Paul stepped in and stuck up for free enterprise and said that we should bring a big mirror and put in front of this Senate committee, for they are the problem. He said that they should be commending Apple for creating over 600,000 jobs in the US. instead of chastising them for the jobs they felt forced to bring elsewhere as well, just to survive. Rand Paul was great, but we have too few people like him who understand free enterprise, and too many critics.

All of us should be free to mind our own businesses.

Ten to Defend

Tommy Brann's "Bill of Rights" in Support of the Free Enterprise System in the United States, as expressed at the Rally for Free Enterprise on Dec. 12, 2011, at Rosa Parks Circle in downtown Grand Rapids:

1. Creating jobs is a compassionate thing to do.

2. Billions of dollars are paid by Free Enterprise when an entrepreneur owns a commercial building and pays property taxes. This helps support local schools, police and fire departments and other community assets.

3. The employer and employee are the backbone of Free Enterprise. Three's a crowd, so government can sometimes get in the way.

4. Anyone with a good work ethic who makes an honest effort can participate in Free Enterprise.

5. Free Enterprise even provides for the unemployed. Businesses pay 100 percent of unemployment insurance.

6. Michael Jordan, the best basketball player ever, is often applauded because of his skills. Successful business people should be applauded, too. We don't take away from Jordan's accomplishments; please don't take away our successful accomplishments as small-business owners.

7. Free Enterprise is not free – participants work hard to create jobs and income by spending long hours away from their families working hard to make sure they can meet an employee payroll.

8. For every hour a person works in a Free Enterprise business, a portion of their Social Security and Medicare taxes are paid by the business owner.

9. When Apple Inc. co-founder Steve Jobs was 24 years old, he told his girlfriend he was going to become a millionaire someday. Free Enterprise is for dreamers – don't take that dream away or America's future will be a nightmare.

10. After Steve Jobs died, admirers laid flowers at his home. They respected him as a businessman and as a participant in Free Enterprise.

THAT IS THE AMERICA THAT I LOVE!

"A dream doesn't become reality through magic. It takes sweat, determination and hard work."
—Colin Powell

Chapter 17:
More Than One Dream

As I write this final chapter, I am sitting at my cottage on Lake Michigan.

Yes, it was a dream of mine when I started my business to own a cottage on Lake Michigan. Ironically, as I sit here, 40 years later, in this place that I set up for relaxation, I am still thinking about my restaurant, my baby. It's Sunday afternoon and I'm wondering, "Are my steaks going out sizzling? Is there any drama with the servers? Is there anything going out the back door?" I know, I know ... what kind of life is that? It's my own fault, though, because my business took over my life. I even feel a little guilty for not being at the restaurant greeting my customers right now. Maybe it's fitting, though, that I'm minding my business even when I'm away, because if it weren't for the countless hours and months and years of work that I put in, I wouldn't have this cottage to come to.

My advice is to follow a lot of the suggestions I've made in this book, but also to have more than one dream in life.

To open a small business at age 19 with $5,000-per-month payments was pretty brave. Not pursuing some of my other dreams earlier in life was not. I hid behind my baby and used my devotion to it as an excuse for not pursuing other dreams, although, in reality, my baby gave me more opportunities than most people get.

I am 60 years old and I am finally stepping out on my baby, the restaurant I opened July 5, 1971, for a change, by serving my country in a small way with the Michigan Volunteer Defense Force.

You can have more than one dream. My focus was just on my restaurant. I didn't make every right decision when I was younger. I want to share with everyone some things I didn't do. I didn't serve in the military and I always felt bad about that, guilty about that, really. I thought about being a police officer at one point. All those American soldiers fought in Vietnam and I was at my restaurant working, but was I doing anything as brave as them? No. I was creating jobs and I was paying taxes, so that's a small consolation.

Having more than one dream allows you to achieve multiple goals. Even if you have a family, it doesn't mean you have to give up other interests. I did that and now I'm trying to make it up. Joining the Michigan Volunteer Defense Force came about because of my regret over not participating in the military in my younger years. I went to Vern Ehlers, former U.S. Representative for Michigan's 3rd congressional district, and I asked him if there was any way I could join the military when I was in my late 50s. Since I was older, there was no reason for me to do so, he told me.

I could join the civil defense and get paid, like an engineer, but what do I know about engineering? One of his suggestions was the Michigan Volunteer Defense Force, which is a military unit in Michigan, formed in 1917. You are part of the military and you get a uniform, and I tell you, I swear, I didn't want to wear that uniform because I didn't think I had earned it. I still have problems when I wear it, but I'm commanded to wear it since I'm a specialist in the Michigan Volunteer Defense Force.

I never pretend to be a Special Forces soldier in Iraq and I never pretend to be a Vietnam veteran. I would never compare myself to those people, but I am doing the very best that I can. In my way, I'm serving. Part of our mission is to secure and store vaccines should Michigan ever be part of a terrorist attack.

I also have served in a number of other ways in the past several years.

I have been a member of the Michigan Restaurant Association Board, past chairman of the Wyoming/Kentwood Chamber of Commerce, chair of the Grand Rapids Community College Culinary Advisory Board for two years, past chairman of the Wyoming Census, EDC vice president, president of the Division Avenue Business Association, and Metro Foundation board member. I'm catching up late in my life.

Ten years ago, I started doing a bunch of stuff. You could call it paying back. It's just serving more. I'm not trying to be a martyr, but just because you're young and focused doesn't mean you should give up on other dreams. Let's say you have a small business, it might be a hardware store, you still have that business but you can go out and climb Mt. Everest. You can get your wife to watch the hardware store for a week and still do it.

It's about being smarter and delegating more. Ronald Reagan was a great President and Jimmy Carter wasn't. Not that they're not both good people, but I have a little Jimmy Carter in me because I didn't delegate enough. Ronald Reagan was a great delegator. Jimmy Carter actually was so hands-on, and I see this in myself, he would have appointments for the tennis courts and he would keep track of playing time on the White House courts. That's how hands-on he was. I mean wouldn't there be bigger and better things for the President of the United States to be doing than scheduling tennis matches? Of course.

Sometimes, I'm still that way. I'm still that hands-on, detail-oriented man. I think it's important in my business to be that way, but it's a lesson that goes both ways. I think you should have a little bit of both. You should have a little bit of the front-line mentality, but still keep the overall bigger picture in mind.

I used to clean my fryers out and my stoves on Sundays when we'd close. I'd take each of the grills, put them outside, and hose them all off. I loved it. We were closed; I got my grills clean, all the grease cleaned off. That was hands-on. I don't do that anymore. I have backed away from some of the smaller details, but they're still getting done. I probably could've learned how to back away from some of that stuff sooner. It gets back to a little bit of paranoia in business. I still think it's healthy and good, but if you have too much paranoia – you're worried about scheduling tennis lessons – maybe instead I should be out talking to 50 people reminding them, "Hey, you should come to Brann's," since that's the bigger picture.

Other times, I fool myself. I don't mean that in a bad way, I know in my 42 years in business, I'm unique. I donated $15,000 to Veterans Park in Grand Rapids. Was it ego? Yeah, it was. You can't run away from ego. Everyone should have an ego. If you didn't, it would be bad for you. It's also a tax deduction; that's a part of it. Overall, I've gotten a lot out of my so-called charitable actions, and I feel proud of what I've done because I chose projects based on my personal areas of interest and belief. Everything I did, I wanted to do.

The Veteran's Park gift was a natural because I didn't serve, and this was my way of recognizing the sacrifice of those who did and showing my respect.

I also bought helmets for the Wyoming Police Department. I always wondered why the Wyoming Police Department – after one of its officers had been fatally shot in the head in the line of duty – didn't have helmets. I mean, you play football and you have a helmet. These are guns. The SWAT team has helmets, but the regular police officers are normally the first responders.

I thought about it and I called the police department and I asked them about it.

They told me, "We're looking at that, but we just don't have the money in our budget." That's when I decided to get involved. I spent $7,500 for them. I wouldn't buy $75 worth of ballerina shoes for the Grand Rapids Ballet because it's just not something I'm interested in. The helmets I bought for the police officers is something I cared about, something I wanted to do, and something I could afford to do. It just came naturally. Even when it's a charitable act, I think the best way to choose your projects is to find a cause that speaks to your own interests. If your heart's not in it, it doesn't have the same effect. This issue was important to me, so now each police car in Wyoming has one helmet in the trunk. No, I don't have Brann's bumper stickers on them. I'm not doing it to get publicity.

I think it's a lesson learned without saying "giving back" so much, which sounds kind of corny. It's opportunity. If you're a small business and you work hard, it's opportunity. It gives you the opportunity to do more for other people in the community where you live and own your small business. And that's better than "giving back,"...as long as you do it the right way.

I'm proud of some other things I've had the opportunity to do for other people because of the success of my business.

We cooked 400 steaks for veterans in July of 2012 and we had a great time doing it because that's something we wanted to do. Again, no offense to the museum, but I wouldn't be cooking 400 steaks for the museum. I don't like being a phony. I have to desire to do these things. I've given a speech and talked in front of 200 people. If it's something you believe in, it's easy. If you're doing it for any other reason, it's going to show through in one way or another. I don't like hypocritical people. I'm sure I've done it like that sometimes, but if I catch myself doing that, I'll pull back.

The Veterans Park, you get a blurb in the paper. Forget about that. When I say ego, I know how hard I've worked in my restaurant for the past 42 years. I want my name to hang around long after I'm gone, so the reason I am able to do these things for others is because I've worked very hard in the free enterprise system.

I remember falling asleep in the front lobby of my restaurant because I was so exhausted. I remember everything I've done in this business. I won't forget it. No offense, but I don't want anybody else to forget it either. I want people to remember this guy, Tommy Brann, and say, "He was a hard worker. I saw him at the rush, I saw him bus tables, I saw him take the trash out. He's a real person."

I started the "You Deserve a Break Today" program in my restaurant.

I borrowed that catchphrase from McDonald's. I put an article in the newspaper for people to come in and have dinner on me if they're going through hard times. I give our waitresses a 35-percent tip out of my pocket, so they liked waiting on these people. It's so cool, I like doing that. I just came up with it.

I've always considered myself an idea person. About three years ago, I wrote an article that said, "You deserve a break today," and anyone who has cancer, or can't make a house payment, or is having hard luck in life can submit their stories to me for consideration to have a meal on me.

I got calls from Hudsonville, Jenison, Grand Rapids, all over the area. I didn't say no to anybody.

They'd write letters and I'd have to call them back and set up the reservation. Usually, it was people who'd write in for other people. That part was cool. Then I'd say, "You'll be my helper, too." Other people would tell me, "She's raising her kids by herself," or "She's hardly making it," and I'd explain the program and say, "Let's make it happen." I'm going to keep doing it. I do it every year. It's a great thing.

The problem was managing the program. I tried to get through to everybody who had left a message or shared their story about hardship. Sometimes, they didn't call back. I had 40 families one year and they all came. Some were two people, some were 10, it didn't matter. They could get anything they wanted. They could get cocktails, no problem. I'd pay for it. I had the food there, I pay wholesale prices.

I'm not trying to be a big martyr here. It's an opportunity to do it, my waitresses loved it, it worked out well.

The people had tears in their eyes when they showed up for dinner at my restaurant. It made their day. It gave them a chance to get out and be with their family when they couldn't afford to do so. Frankly, it kind of made my day too.

If you put profit with opportunity, they're both great words.

Although business is interpreted as a cold word sometimes, the combination of business, profit, and opportunity together is what made "You Deserve a Break Today" possible. The program has all of the elements that make everything possible. If you unleash free enterprise, a lot of small-business owners will do the right thing.

I'm sure I'm not the only person in business who participates in acts of kindness.

I truly believe that you can accomplish anything through hard work. I'm proof of that.

It all sounds impressive, all of these things I've accomplished, all of these opportunities I've been afforded to help make a difference, but, to me, my most impressive accomplishment as a small-business owner has been creating jobs for other people. Creating a job is one of the most compassionate things you can do for someone.

If you do, just be prepared to mind your own business.

About the Author

Tommy Brann, called "the hardest working restaurateur in the world," has been in the restaurant business since the age of 17, opening his restaurant, Tommy Brann's Sizzling Steaks and Sports Grille in Wyoming, Michigan, at the age of 19.

Mr. Brann has served in many leadership positions at the city, county and state levels. Among these positions are President of the Division Ave. Business Association, 9 year board member Michigan Restaurant Association, Grand Rapids Community College Advisory Board for the culinary division, Wyoming-Kentwood Chamber of Commerce, Chair of Godwin Heights Advisory Committee, Chair of 2000 Wyoming Census, Gateway Project innovator, Grand Rapids Chamber of Commerce tax advisory committee, and current Vice President of Wyoming EDC economic development corporation.

He has received many awards and commendations: a black belt in Karate, Grand Rapids Community College Culinary Hall of Fame recipient, Wyoming-Kentwood Chamber Gerald E. Fessell Distinguished Service Award, Michigan Restaurant Association distinguished service award recipient, 12-gallon blood donor, and a Specialist in the Michigan Volunteer Defense Force.

Now CEO of Brann's Steakhouse and Sports Grille, he remains involved in all aspects of the restaurant business. He lives and works in Wyoming, Michigan with his wife Sue and their beloved dog, Howie.

Mr. Brann is available to speak to your class, club, group or organization.

Please contact him at tombrann@branns.com.

About the Writer

Brian Van Ochten first met Tommy Brann while living the dream as an award-winning sports columnist and highly respected local radio personality. He formed an instant and everlasting friendship with him. They share the same common-sense approach to life, business and the pursuit of happiness. And, of course, an affinity for man's best friend.

He spent much of his professional career at The Grand Rapids Press and MLive.com, covering all four major-league sports franchises in Detroit, Big Ten Conference football and basketball, Notre Dame football and everything possible on the local landscape. Currently he is the business editor at The Holland Sentinel, feature writer for Stellafly Social Media and founder of Angel Wings multimedia brand management, specializing in public relations, marketing and social media services.